"O Lord, I'm Single Again!"

(So Now What?)

Dr. Dennis Henderson

SINGLE INITIATIVE

"All for the glory of God"

"O Lord, I'm Single Again!" (So Now What?)

Copyright © 2014 by Dennis L. Henderson
Published by Single Initiative, LLC
2909 Summervale Lane
Bloomfield Hills, MI 48301

Formerly released under the title:
Hope for New Relationships
A Case Study of Friendship and Strength
Copyright © 2008 by Dennis L Henderson
Published by Single Initiative, LLC

"All for the glory of God"

Library of Congress Catalog Card Number: 2008904911
Printed in the United States of America

First Printing: August 2008
Second Retitled Printing: 2014

All scripture quotations, unless otherwise indicated, are taken from the HOLY BIBLE, NEW INTERNATIONAL VERSION®. NIV®. Copyright © 1973, 1978, 1984 by International Bible Society. Used by permission of Zondervan. All rights reserved.

Scripture quotations marked NLT are taken from the Holy Bible, New Living Translation, copyright 1996, 2004. Used by permission of Tyndale House Publishers, Inc., Wheaton, Illinois 60189. All rights reserved.

Library of Congress Cataloging-in-Publication Data
Henderson, Dennis
"O Lord, I'm Single Again!" (So Now What?)

ISBN 978-0-9818236-1-4
Cover design by: Dennis Henderson

Contents

Charts

Abbreviations

BDB — Brown Driver and Briggs (Oxford Press)
NIV — New International Version (Zondervan)
KJV — King James Version of the Holy Bible
NET — New English Translation (www.bible.org)
NLT — New Living Translation (Tyndale House)
TWOT — Theological Wordbook of the Old
          Testament (Moody Press)

Preface

O Lord, I'm Single Again grew out of the need for single-again people, after divorce or grief recovery, to develop hope for future relationships from a solid Biblical foundation. From the beginning the desire was to do a case study of Bible characters that were single or single again, to gain hope from the way they developed relationships that lasted. That focus led to the little book of Ruth in which the storyline included characters who either became single again or were already single. This book is a case study of the main characters in the book of Ruth, with remarks directed specifically to the single and single-again person. The goal here is not simply to write about the Bible or Bible characters but rather to see how both the singles and single-again people in the Bible built relationships that lasted and use them as a model for living single today.

The goal of this case study is to develop a Biblical framework in which to build future relationships that will last a lifetime. This will offer hope. The Biblical concept of hope is more than "wishful thinking"; it is a "confident assurance." Most single-again people do not have a confident assurance that the next relationship will last. That's because most people today do not have a Biblical foundation for relationships. Because they do not, they only have a wishful thinking that the next relationship will last—not the confident assurance that it will last.

Having been a single-again person myself, I must admit that it took a long while before I could say I was grateful for the circumstance in my life that led to becoming single again. Through my divorce recovery period, God providentially brought so many wonderful single people into my life. I am grateful to the many single and single-again people who helped shape my heart and mind to the great need for Singles' Ministry. I am deeply thankful for my close friend, Jim Coram, who repeatedly asked me, "Isn't there something that will take us past divorce recovery?" That repeated question led to the development of the seven-part DVD video series *Living Single Again* which has been offered in hundreds of churches nationally. (*Living Single Again* is available online at www.LivingSingleAgain.com). The *Living Single Again* video series is a topical treatment on how to develop new relationships that will last for a lifetime. Even with the success of *Living Single Again*, there still remained the need to develop a case study of what a healthy single and single-again life would look like from within the Bible. It is from that need that this book was written.

Gratitude is extended to all who helped with this work. I thank my wife, Dianne, who prodded me along, both to begin writing and to persevere to the end. I am grateful to Chuck Jones, Singles Director of the Church Street United Methodist Church in Knoxville, TN and Don Pedde, Campus Pastor of the Woodside Bible Church of Warren, MI who invited me to offer the contents of this book as four-part case study lecture series to their singles ministry groups. The many questions from each group helped clarify the final outcome of this book. Special thanks to those who read the manuscript and offered so many valuable suggestions. Allow me to thank Doris Bryant, Kathy Coram, Don Pedde, and Cindy Romeos.

To my wife, Dianne,
whose friendship strengthens
me and makes her such
a wonderful wife.

"O Lord, I'm Single Again!"

Part 1:
"Lord, Where are You When I Need You?

With the sound of crunching gravel under my tires, I pulled onto the gravel driveway that led to our Dutch Colonial house and slammed my car's gear shifter into park. I made a fist, pounded the dashboard, and then cried out, "God, why is this happening to me?" My wife had asked me for a divorce and consequently the board of the church where I served as pastor had asked me to resign. I was losing my marriage, family, friends, and career. It was like a famine had struck my life and everything important to me was withering away as my faith was being challenged beyond anything I had ever known.

It wasn't always like that. Just a year earlier I pulled into that same driveway with the same sound of gravel crunching under my tires, but as I came to a stop, just in front of the garage doors, a sensation of blessing had overwhelmed me. I paused and spoke out, "Lord, you have really blessed my life. I have a spacious home, a loving wife, two teenage sons and one preteen son who love You. Thank You Lord for the unusual growth spurt at church as well. Lord, so much is going right, there's little that demands my trust in You ...." You see, God had filled my life with so many blessings that I just wanted to acknowledge them and thank Him. You might say that during that previous year I had been living in the house of God's blessing. I must admit that it was easy to live there. The truth is that's where we all want to live—all the time. But I wasn't living in the past anymore. Famine struck my life and everything changed. I knew my life was not going to be easy from that point on!

This book is a case study in *living single again*. I am not the case that will be studied, but I will interrupt this case study from time to time to share my "single-again" story. The case that will be studied comes from the lives of three people who experience living "single again" and one "never married single." They are the people described in the little book of Ruth[1] found in the Old Testament of the Bible.

When Times Are Tough

> **I have yet to meet the single-again person who could claim that the timing of the divorce or death was perfect! It never is.**

One of Murphy's laws says, If anything can go wrong it will, at the most inopportune time. I have yet to meet the single-again person who could claim that the timing of the divorce or death was perfect! It never is. Likewise, the times were tough when the case study took place. It begins with a single sentence that tells us *when* it took place, *what* was happening at that time, and *where* it all happened. It says ...

Ruth 1:1 In the days when the judges ruled, there was a famine in the land....

This case study took place "In the days *when* the judges ruled."[2] They were dark and dismal days in many ways. Most notably, they were dark spiritually. The previous book of the Bible, called the Judges (because it tells the story of 12 judges who ruled in the land in those days), is characterized by constant rebellion against God. Common are expressions like, "Then the Israelites did evil in the eyes of the LORD," or they "served the Baals" (false gods), or "they forsook the LORD," or they "worshiped various gods," or "they provoked the LORD to anger." At one point in the story God was so frustrated with his people, He said, "You have forsaken me and served other gods, so I will no longer save you. Go and cry out to the gods you have chosen. Let them save you when you are in trouble!" (Judges 10:13, 14). Spiritually times were tough.

It is no different now. When we forsake the Lord and go after the gods of our age, we too find that the Lord grows weary with us. Those of us who have been believers for a significant length of time have felt that cold darkness fall over our spirits when we have rebelled against the Lord. The longer we stay in that darkness, the deeper and darker it gets. Well, our case study takes place in those days that were very dark spiritually. It is all summed up in a single verse in Judges 21:25 "Everyone did as he saw fit." Not as God desired, but as each man chose to do.

Just like our 21st century global condition of terrorism, war, fear, and the like, the days of the case study were dark days politically, too. Judges 2:14 says, "Because they forsook him.... the LORD handed them over to raiders who plundered them. He sold them to their enemies all around, whom they were no longer able to resist." They were terrorized by oppressors who plundered their goods and enslaved them. They experienced the severe hardships of living in a war-torn land. It really was in times like ours that this case study took place. Politically, times were tough.

Obviously the days were dark emotionally as well. Fear, grief, sorrow, and emotional pain reigned as they lived in constant fear of war, oppression, enslavement, and the deaths of loved ones. Times were emotionally tough.

On top of all that, "There was a famine in the land." This famine may have been the result of the chastening hand of God for their rebellious disposition, or it may have been just coincidental. The study does not say. Either way, it was real. Either way, it touched them where they lived. They were hungry—perhaps starving. Most readers have never experienced this kind of hunger from famine. But many have experienced famine in other ways: financially, emotionally, spiritually, and relationally. The single-again person reading this knows the pangs of pain that come from the loss of a relationship, whether by death or divorce. He or she knows what it is to live on an empty "love tank" either before the divorce or after the death of a spouse. He or she has experienced the starvation of the love he or she once knew. That love was either intentionally withheld from them by the "ex" or taken away from them by death. Yes, he or she knows famine of a different sort than just food, and perhaps in an even more severe form. It affects not just the body, but the heart, soul, mind—the whole person.

The place where the famine hit, according to this case study, is simply stated as "in the land." Of course, "the land" for God's Old Testament people, Israel, was the land that God had promised Abraham and his descendants—Canaan.[3] It was a land that flowed with "milk and honey"[4] (an idiom for prosperity and blessing). But more importantly, it carried with it the idea of "being in the place where God wanted them." It was to live in God's will. To be out of the land was to be out of God's will (unless of course it was on one of those rare occasions in which God specifically told His people to go out of the land).[5] In this case study, no such summon to leave the land was given by God. It was God's will to be in the land.

I think we can all identify with this. We who know Christ, know where He wants us. God has given us His Word, the Bible, where He makes His will known. He has likewise given us His Spirit Who bears witness with our spirits regarding His will when we read the Bible. We who genuinely know Christ as Savior also know that uneasy feeling we get from the inner witness of God's Spirit with our spirit, when we are not where God wants us to be. When we are not in the land of His will but in the land of our will, there is a sense of uneasiness and an inner struggle for peace that is ever elusive.

So the opening line of this case study has established *when* this case study happened (during the time of the Judges), *what* made it happen (famine), and *where* it happened (in the land). Next the case study introduces a rather ambiguous character simply called "a man." The ambiguity of calling him just "a man" at this point leads us to believe that it could be any man. It could have been you or me, caught in the famine of life, had we lived at that time. Of course, as we have already seen, famines come in our times as well. So we are invited to identify with this man. Now he is not just any man, he is a specific individual, as we are specific individuals. He had a home town, as we have a home town. He had a real family, as we have a real family.

This man is said to be "a man from Bethlehem in Judah." The significance of this is immense. All the names of this case study are significant because God, in His divine providence, has shaped both the place names and peoples' names to add to the story, as it unfolds. For example, the name "Bethlehem," in Hebrew, means "House of Bread."[6] The name itself adds to the story by suggesting that the land in which the man lived ought to be a place of feasting—not famine. The man should be living in God's prosperity because he lived in "Bethlehem, Judah."

The name "Judah," in Hebrew, means "Praise."[7] Of course, it is easy to give praise when your stomach is full and when life itself is full. It is easy to praise God when you dwell in the house of bread and live in prosperity. I was, "in the land"—when I first drove into my driveway contemplating all God's

> **Of course it is easy to give praise when life is full. The question you must ask yourself is, "What hope is there when fullness turns to emptiness?"**

blessings in my life. Now here's the rub. This man who lived in the land called the "House of Bread" (in the land of "prosperity") was confronted with the reality of a severe famine. Not only did he experience famine, but so did his family who depended on him. The verse goes on to say: "together with his wife and two sons."

They were all hungry for more. Perhaps as you read this, you too can identify with the desire for more from life. Not just more stuff—but more or better relationships. The question you must ask yourself is, "What hope is there when fullness turns to emptiness?" "Where can you turn when good times go bad?" "What can you do when your House of Bread turns to famine?" Or even more pointedly ...

"Lord, Where are You When I Need You?"

When things are not going right, we begin to doubt, blame, and question. The man of this case study is not unlike us at all. He did just as we too frequently do. Too often when we see the slightest sign of famine coming, we choose to abandon God, His church, and the path of righteousness. We may even say or think, "Lord, where are You when I need You?" We aren't told if the "man" of this case study asked that, but He did choose to flee the promised "land" of blessing, the "House of Bread," in order to go to "live for a while in the country of Moab."

Notice that his goal was to leave the "House of Bread" for "a little while." The aberration from God's will was to be only temporary—not permanent. We also tell ourselves some of the most convincing lies when we want to leave God's will to do our own thing. We tell ourselves that we will not remain outside His will forever—just temporarily. Once we have fixed things, then we will return (as if God cannot fix them). Moab sounded reasonable to him because in Moab there was food, while in the "House of Bread" there was famine.

It is important to note that even the name "Moab" is

14

significant. The word "Moab" means "from father."[8] The "father" of the Moabites was a man named "Lot."[9] Lot, as you may recall, was a man who was set on living in godless Sodom,[10] whose wife turned to a pillar of salt for looking back to the old life,[11] and whose oldest daughter, after the destruction of Sodom, slept with him and gave him a son called Moab.[12] So it is clear that what came "from this father" (i.e. Lot) was a legacy of destruction, death, and despair. What a shame that the man of the case study who was from the "House of Bread," in the land of promise, went to the land of destruction, death, and despair. What a backslide.

Meet the Family

Up to this point, the case study has not revealed the name of the man, but now he is identified. His family is identified as well. So let's meet the family.

Ruth 1:2 The man's name was Elimelech, his wife's name Naomi, and the names of his two sons were Mahlon and Kilion. They were Ephrathites from Bethlehem, Judah. And they went to Moab and lived there.

Elimelech is the man's name and it means "My God is King."[13] How sad! How ironic. His name was a declarative sentence that proclaimed "My God is King." That implied that he was God's subject, and as such, it was his duty to do the King's will—but his actions proved to the contrary. You might say that he was a hypocrite, in the fullest sense of

Rather than endure the hardship of famine that God brought into his life as a test of his faith—he sought to escape God's testing and to take the easy way out.

the word. He was no different from the other men of his day for he "did as he saw fit"—not as God saw fit (see Judges 17:6; 21:25). You see, rather than endure the hardship of famine that God brought into his life as a test of his faith—he sought to escape God's testing and to take the easy way out by temporarily fleeing to the greener grass of Moab.

He may have started out to dwell temporarily outside "the land," but did you notice that the case study flat out records that a different attitude soon set in? It says that they "lived there." Sounds rather permanent, doesn't it? Temporary disobedience to the will of his King had a funny way of becoming a permanent addiction. Just ask any alcoholic or person with any addiction. One little drink or one use of a drug leads to another. One disobedience to God's will, unchecked, leads to another.

His wife's name was "Naomi," which means "My Pleasantness."[14] Obviously, living in the land of promised blessing, in the "House of Bread," would be a pleasant experience. The possessive pronoun, "My," in her name, "My Pleasantness," jumps off the page as a suggestion that she actually possessed "happiness." Happiness had been hers. Perhaps she was "happily married" or perhaps she had a "happy family" life. Whatever it was that she possessed, this case study was written to lead us to believe that "life was good and she was pleased." Everyone can think of a time when they were happy—so we can easily identify with her, too.

Elimelech ("My God is King") and Naomi ("My Pleasantness") had two sons: one named "Mahlon," which means "sickly,"[15] and the other, "Kilion," which means "pining" or "wasting away."[16] Not only do these two names suggest that not all was well in the family (both names suggest the boys had health issues), but the names, as the case study unfolds, will become self-fulfilling prophesies. Both will die prematurely by all normal standards.

The members of this family are "Ephrathites" because they are from the region of Ephratha, which means "fruitful."[17] Are you noticing that this case study has deliberately piled up names with profound significance to describe that they left the land of God's blessing, the land of "fruitfulness" in the "House of Bread" for the land of Moab (destruction, death, and despair)? That's what we do too, when we "temporarily" leave God's will to do our own thing.

The Crisis—"Becoming Single Again"

By the third verse of this case study, the man whose name meant "My God is King," but whose actions were quite the contrary, died. He did so outside the "House of Bread" in the foreign land that truly was a land of destruction to him. The Bible says…

Ruth 1:3 Now Elimelech, Naomi's husband, died, and she was left with her two sons.

So Naomi, whose name means "My pleasantness," found herself anything but pleasant. She found herself living single again as a bereft, single-again mom with two boys in a foreign land that had already taken its toll on her life. Most widows reading this can feel her pain from her loss and truly identify with her in this scenario.

Of course not all was gloom for Naomi. As the boys matured they met Moabite women, fell in love with Moabite women, and as a result …

1:4 They married Moabite women, one named Orpah and the other Ruth.

Naomi had become the mother of the groom at two weddings. However, both her two sons took wives from the Moabites. This too may have been an aberration from what God desired for their lives. In light of other passages of Scripture, a case could be made that the Jews were not to take wives of foreigners (See Genesis 28:1, 6; Ezra 10:11), yet they

17

did and of course their brides' names are significant for this case study. The name of the one bride was "Orpah," which means "back or neck."[18] In both Exodus and Joshua, Orpah's name was used as a common noun for the concept of "retreat,"[19] and is used elsewhere in the expression "stiff-necked." [20]

The other bride was named "Ruth," which means "friendship."[21] These names will become self-fulfilling prophesies, as will be seen with the unfolding of this case study.

Three Choices Confronting All Single-Again People

1:4 After they had lived there about ten years, 5 both Mahlon and Kilion also died, and Naomi was left without her two sons and her husband.

Ten years passed and Naomi's two sons died. Their deaths forced both Orpah and Ruth into "living single again" as widows, just like Naomi. Now the rest of this study will focus on how these three women coped with living single again. Orpah will go back into the old life, Naomi will turn bitter, and Ruth will get better. These are the three choices that all living single-again people have, whether by death or divorce. You can either go back to your old life, become bitter about your present life, or you can go on to a better life. The choices are stark in contrast.

> **Orpah will go back into the old life, Naomi will turn bitter, and Ruth will get better. These are the three choices that all living single-again people have.**

Life is not easy when we experience a famine. Often we attempt to move to the greener grass on the other side, only to have our heart ripped out. That was Naomi's story. That was her daughters-in-law story too. In spite of all their pain, there was no "time out" in real life. There was no putting life on hold to get a second wind. Choices had to be made. After all, what would they do? How would they live? Where would they live? How would they support themselves? Choices had to be made.

So what influences our choices? The same things that influenced the choices of these three women: current circumstances, assessment of what appeared to be the best possible prospect for the future, and the counsel of family and friends.

There is one thing about circumstances that you can count on—they always change. They did for Naomi. Good news came to her from her hometown:

1:6 … she heard in Moab that the LORD had come to the aid of his people by providing food for them.

Subtly tucked away in this verse is the answer to the question, "Where is God when you need Him?" He was right where Naomi had left Him! He was, so to speak, back in the land of blessing in the "House of Bread." The Lord had not left! Naomi had left. When we feel abandoned and are prone to ask, "Lord, where are You?" We may want to just retrace our steps to see where *we* departed. He had not left. In fact, you might say the Lord had stayed in the land to replenish the pantry in the "House of Bread" (Bethlehem). So much for the so-called "greener grass of Moab." Well, this good news, and the prospect of a brighter future, was the prime influencer for her to make her next move:

1:6 Naomi and her daughters-in-law prepared to return home from there.

19

"Returning home" was a no-brainer! Home was now a secure place. Moab was not safe anymore. But with the visitation of God's blessing, Bethlehem was. There is a sense in which "returning home," for Naomi, was returning to the Lord and His will. Being in God's will is always a safe place, no matter how desperate the famine may be. Those who had not left Bethlehem for Moab were already reaping the blessings of their endurance and perseverance. In any case, for Naomi, "returning home" was the best move she could make in the journey of living single again. The same is true for us today. No matter where you have been, "returning home" to the Lord is the best move you can make.

1:7 With her two daughters-in-law she left the place where she had been living and set out on the road that would take them back to the land of Judah.

Both daughters-in-law set out with Naomi. No doubt, they too were influenced by the good news and the prospect of a better life than what Moab had dealt them. But would that be the best choice for them as well? After all, Bethlehem was not "home" for either of them. They were Moabites.

1:8 Then Naomi said to her two daughters-in-law, "Go back, each of you, to your mother's home...."

The two daughters-in-law were at a crossroad. They could stay in Moab, the land of destruction, death, and despair, or they could venture on to "Bethlehem," the "House of Bread." You might say that the table was now turned on them. Elimelech, had left Bethlehem for Moab. Now the question was, "Will they really leave Moab for Bethlehem?" "Will they really leave their mother's home?"

Many people, after a crisis, start on a noble path, but they don't last long. They often say, "This time it will be different. I'm *not* going to repeat the same mistake again. This time I'm turning over a new leaf. This is going to be a fresh start." Now, common sense tells us there are two ingredients for making change last. First, it takes repetitive *practice* of the new course of action. Second, it takes *time* to repeat the action over and over to make it stick. You can tell yourself, "This time I'm going to change," but unless you practice the new life-style repetitiously over an extended period of time, it's not going to stick. You can be sure that temptation will arise, both from within and without, that will entice you to go back to doing what you did before. But what you did before did not work. You see, without an incredible resolve to live out the new changes over an extended period of time, the new changes will fall by the wayside. You can be sure that if your resolve is a good one, it will be challenged by someone. Some people will flat out scorn you for attempting a new noble ambition while others will challenge your resolve. They will say, "Do you really think you can do that?" Naomi challenged the resolve of her daughters-in-law.

1:8 ... "May the LORD show kindness to you, as you have shown to your dead and to me. 9 May the LORD grant that each of you will find rest in the home of another husband...."

Naomi was sincere when she invoked God to show kindness and bless her daughters-in-law with finding new husbands. That's what would make the act of quitting sound so reasonable for Orpah and Ruth. No doubt just hearing Naomi say "Go back" would have removed some of the obligation they sensed was theirs, to take care of their widowed mother-in-law. Still the two daughters-in-law did the politically correct thing (at least the family-correct thing). They asserted their resolve...

1:10 And they said to her, "We will go back with you to your people."

So Naomi challenged their resolve even more pointedly. She said:

1:11 "...Return home, my daughters. Why would you come with me? Am I going to have any more sons, who could become your husbands? 12 Return home, my daughters; I am too old to have another husband. Even if I thought there was still hope for me—even if I had a husband tonight and then gave birth to sons—13 would you wait until they grew up? Would you remain unmarried for them? No, my daughters. It is more bitter for me than for you, because the LORD's hand has gone out against me!"

Naomi really pressed her daughters-in-law resolve with the fact that she had absolutely nothing to offer them. It appears that Naomi was appealing to her daughters-in-law sense of self-preservation. She was basically saying, "Look out for yourself and forget about me." It is so easy, in a crisis, to take the attitude of a martyr and pretend that you can go it alone. That's what Naomi had done. She even heightened the stakes by saying that if you join me, you are placing yourself under the "hand of God," which she was certain had gone out against her. Why would anyone want to join a loser?

Naomi was counting on this deterrence to dissuade her daughters-in-law from going back to Bethlehem with her. She had chosen a path of self-incrimination, depression, anger, and bitterness. It appears that the more she tried to convince her daughters-in-law to leave her, the more bitter she was becoming.

Singles Standing at a Crossroad

Every single-again person stands at a crossroad the moment they become single again,. They ask themselves, "Which way will I go with what is left of my life?" Likewise,

Naomi's daughters-in-law were also standing at a crossroad. They must decide which way to go. Forward or backward? The case study says:

1:14 At this they wept again. Then Orpah kissed her mother-in-law good-by, but Ruth clung to her.

Orpah, did just what her name signified, she went "back." She retreated. She fled. She represents all who turn back; all who don't keep their resolve. She pictures those who are more comfortable with old life than gaining a new one. She is like all those well-intending divorce recovery or grief recovery drop-outs who go back to the old life. Her resolve to move on and get better was very short-lived.

Every divorce recovery group has watched some single-again people drop out. Most frequently single-again people drop out of the resolve to complete recovery and replace it with a "new relationship." That's exactly what Naomi was suggesting that Orpah and Ruth do—find someone else. This is still the number one tidbit offered by "pop coun-selors," family and friends: "You just need to get on with your life, so find someone new—someone better."

It's strange that single-again people believe that if they just had that "new relationship" all the pain would go away. But they're wrong. Oh sure, there is some truth that "new relationships" do have the power to temporarily remove the pain—like an anesthesia. But anesthesia doesn't heal, it masks the pain. When a physical wound occurs, anesthesia is used to mask the pain so surgery can be performed to fix the problem. In a similar way, the anesthesia of a "new relationship" will mask the pain—but no

"New relationships" do have the power to temporarily remove the pain. Like an anesthesia. But anesthesia doesn't heal--it masks the pain.

healing surgery occurs. So the latter end is worse than the former. However, there is a better anesthesia than a "new relationship." The better anesthesia is called "recovery group." The anesthesia of a "recovery group" both provides the safe place to make radical changes in your life and offers the support needed for genuine long-lasting healing to occur.

Now in stark contrast to Orpah, this case study says, "but Ruth clung to Naomi." Of course, Naomi was not finished with Ruth either. She probably thought, "One daughter-in-law down and one to go." So she turned her focus on Ruth.

1:15 "Look," said Naomi, "your sister-in-law is going back to her people and her gods. Go back with her."

In Moab both Orpah and Ruth had grown up in an idolatrous environment. Having married Mahlon and Kilion meant taking their husbands' God, the true God, as their own. But now, they were freed to chose for themselves. There is a sense in which every marriage is influenced by the behaviors of the spouse. The spouse influences just about everything, from the friends you hang out with to the music you listen to. From the way you discipline your kids to the things you watch on TV. Of course, like Orpah and Ruth, your former spouse influenced your view of religion and morality.

As with the two Moabite women, there was a "B.M. life" (before marriage) and a married life. When the divorce or death of the relationship occurred, everything changed. You were released from all of your spouse's influences, whether good or bad. You were freed.

The issue then became, "Will you go back to the former life?" Back to the B.M. life? The B.M. life is even more important for the reader whose B.M. life was full of baggage, full of idolatry. Will you go back to the pit from which you were pulled or will you move on? Orpah went back to the pit—to idolatry. She forsook the true and living God to return to her pantheon of gods. I have observed single-again people return to former lifestyles that included the bar scene, promiscuous living, and other pits from which they had come. That is the easy road—it's the one familiar because it was traveled once before. The better road will not be so easy.

The Right Road Is Rarely Easy

You may have gathered that to rise above the pressure to go back to an old life style, you need an absolute commitment and resolve to leave the past and press on to the future. This path is rarely easy. But Ruth had both resolve and commitment. Ruth countered Naomi's persuasive deterrence to leave her with the following rebuttal that showed how resolved and committed she was.

16 "...Don't urge me to leave you or to turn back from you. Where you go I will go, and where you stay I will stay. Your people will be my people and your God my God. [17]Where you die I will die, and there I will be buried. May the LORD deal with me, be it ever so severely, if anything but death separates you and me."

Orpah had made the decision to go back to her "gods," while Ruth made the decision to accept the true and living God. The words of Ruth are often quoted at weddings, as the commitment between a wife and husband. But notice that in this context, Ruth really was speaking to another single woman. She was seeking to have a new lease on life that started with a new relationship with the true living God and with her mother-in-law! These words are her expression of absolute resolve not to "turn back." Those are the two major choices before every single-again person: go back to the old lifestyle of destruction, death, despair and false gods or choose to be like Ruth who chose to get a better life. The choice to get a better life will not necessarily be easy, but it will be rewarding, as the rest of the case study will demonstrate. In the face of such resolve and commitment, Naomi backed off. The case study puts it like this:

1:18 ...Naomi realized that Ruth was determined to go with her, she stopped urging her. 19 So the two women went on until they came to Bethlehem. When they arrived in Bethlehem, the whole town was stirred because of them, and the women exclaimed, "Can this be Naomi?"

It was reported that "the whole town was stirred" when the two returned to the "House of Bread." So it can be safely inferred that when Naomi had originally left Bethlehem for Moab, it was a huge public statement. No doubt, when Elimelech and Naomi were considering leaving Bethlehem for Moab there were questions asked of them by the Bethlehem community. "Why are you leaving?" "Where are you going?" "How long will you be gone?" And, of course, you can imagine how Naomi and Elimelech justified their departure. She and her husband probably said that it would only be temporary and that they were going to secure a more successful and prosperous life in Moab. Can you imagine the crow she now had to eat? What can she say? Moab had been anything but good to her. How many times would she have to repeat her painful story of all that she had lost in Moab?

Isn't that the fear of every single-again person, the fear that everyone will ask, "What happened to you?" Or even harsher, "How could this have happened to you?" We all fear having to dredge it all up again to explain our loss and pain. People say things like, "The two of you were so perfect together." Well, maybe you were, but for most people it was not as perfect as it was thought to be. Many tried to protect what little relationship they had and hoped that by doing so it would get better. Others just didn't want to expose how horribly bad it was. Still, for a small group of others it was really very good. Whatever the case, no one likes to make themselves vulnerable to the "I told you so" pack of wolves.

I recall how ashamed I felt, that as a pastor who taught the sanctity of marriage and that "God hates divorce," I too had experienced the pain of divorce. I felt like such a failure. In fact, there are times that I still do. But when divorce was still fresh and I was really emotionally raw, I just wanted to be a totally ambiguous person. So to find help without being recognized, I traveled miles away to attend a church of a different denomination in order to attend Divorce Recovery. I did not want anyone to know my story. I shared little. I never even told my recovery group that I was a pastor—my shame was too great. I felt like such a failure. It took a long time to face it. Deep down in my soul I still carry a degree of shame, especially when I am among pastors. I do not want anyone to know. Why? A sense of pride on my part perhaps. I am a Christian. I am a pastor. This was not supposed to have happened to me. Likewise, you, the reader, have experienced the same kind of thing. The details that brought about being "single again" may be unique, but the experience of shamefulness is the same.

Naomi was no different, but when asked, "Can this be Naomi?" she chose to confront it head on:

1:20 "Don't call me Naomi," she told them. "Call me Mara, because the Almighty has made my life very bitter. 21 I went away full, but the LORD has brought me back empty. Why call me Naomi? The LORD has afflicted me; the Almighty has brought misfortune upon me."

The question asked by the women, "Can this be Naomi?" only required a "yes" or "no" answer. But Naomi was compelled to give more. Out of her tremendous pain she lashed out, "Don't call me 'My Pleasantness,' call me 'Bitterness.'" The Hebrew name "Mara" meant "bitter-ness."[22] Even Naomi could tell that she had become a bitter old woman. Her bitterness was actually an internalized anger over her severe losses which was a normal part of grieving.

There are five well established stages to grieving the loss of a relationship.

There are five well estab-lished stages to grieving the loss of a relationship which were first identified by Elizabeth Kübler-Ross in her book *On Death and Dying.*[23]

Naomi showed signs of the first stage called *denial,* which normally focuses on a denial of the circumstances. Normally, the grieving person responds to the harsh loss with, "Oh, no! This can't be happening to me." They may even go into shock. This stage is not limited to denial of the circumstances. It may manifest itself in other ways. Naomi manifested her denial by denying her own worthiness to be accompanied by her daughters-in-law when returning to the land and the denial that God would have any blessing in store for her in the future.

Naomi's second stage of grief was *anger.* This stage is so obvious from the case study. Naomi had internalized her anger into both bitterness and depression. She even recognized the severity of it within herself and rightly calls herself "Bitterness."

Naomi's third stage of grief was blaming God for her severe circumstance. Usually the third stage is called *bargaining* because the grieving person bargains with God by pleading something like, "If You would just …, then I would …." The bargaining is an attempt to postpone—but with Naomi the worst had already happened. On top of that, Naomi saw God as the absolutely sovereign Lord who was responsible for her heartache and so it appeared that she blamed Him instead of bargaining with Him. For Naomi it was more like, "You could have…, but you didn't."

The fourth stage of grief is *depression.* Though the case study does not name her state as "depressed," it is obvious that she was severely depressed over her great sense of loss. That loss had its toll on her physically, emotionally, rationally, and spiritually.

The last stage of grieving is *acceptance*. Not until some time later will she come to accept the loss and see God's good hand in any of this (Ruth 2:20).

Now all these stages that she was experiencing were normal reactions for a person grieving the loss of a loved one. Although the stages do not excuse negative behaviors resulting from such loss, they do help us understand her. Everyone who has experienced the loss of a relationship through death or divorce can identify with Naomi's bitterness. Notice that both Orpah and Ruth went through similar loss of a husband, but not loss of children. They however, appear to have recovered much more quickly. All people do not pass through the stages at the same rate. Some choose to move on more quikly. Some get stuck on a stage, while others even slide back into a stage once they leave it.

It appears that Naomi knew that she was stuck in her bitterness. Her newly chosen name "Mara," or "Bitterness," summed up her disposition and described the third possible option to living single again. You see the single-again person can choose to go "back" as Orpah did, or choose to get "bitter" as Naomi did, or choose to get "better" as Ruth did. Those are your three options too.

The truth is, Naomi had become very bitter, and her bitterness distorted everything—beginning with her view of what had happened.

Naomi said, "I went away full." Oh really? Then why did she leave the land if she was so full? Had she forgotten, or had her bitter disposition just rewritten the past? The fact was she went away because there was famine in the land. They were hungry. She was dissatisfied. She was not full. She looked at Moab as a place to be filled—and it turned out to have a very bitter sting in the end.

Naomi also said, "the LORD has brought me back empty." Oh really? How do you suppose that made Ruth, who was standing by her side, feel? Perhaps a little like chopped liver! Ruth, whose name meant "friendship," had chosen to return with her and covenanted to live and die with

Naomi had allowed her bitterness to influence her perspective on God and everything else too.

her. So Naomi had not returned empty-handed. She had acquired a friend that this case study will later say was better than seven sons (4:15).

What had happened to Naomi was that Naomi had allowed her bitterness to influence her perspective on God and everything else too. She said:

1:21 "...the LORD has brought me back empty. Why call me Naomi? The LORD has afflicted me; the Almighty has brought misfortune upon me."

Naomi felt afflicted by God. She was blaming God because she perceived her circumstances as a curse—not a blessing. But was it really a curse as she perceived it or was it a blessing in disguise? An old fable may help us understand this question of curse or blessing:

> Once there was an old man who lived in a tiny village. Although poor, he was envied by all, for he owned a beautiful white horse. Even the king coveted his treasure. A horse like this had never been seen before—such was its splendor, its majesty, its strength.

> People offered fabulous prices for the steed, but the old man always refused. "This horse is not a horse to me," he would tell them. "It is a person. How could you sell a person? He is a friend, not a possession. How could you sell a friend?" The man was poor and the temptation was great. But he never sold the horse.

> One morning he found that the horse was not in the

stable. All the village came to see him. "You old fool," they scoffed, "we told you that someone would steal your horse. We warned you that you would be robbed. You are so poor. How could you ever hope to protect such a valuable animal? It would have been better to have sold him. You could have gotten whatever price you wanted. No amount would have been too high. Now the horse is gone, and you've been cursed with misfortune."

The old man responded, "Don't speak too quickly. Say only that the horse is not in the stable. That is all we know; the rest is judgment. If I've been cursed or not, how can you know? How can you judge?"

The people contested, "Don't make us out to be fools! We may not be philosophers, but great philosophy is not needed. The simple fact that your horse is gone is a curse."

The old man spoke again. "All I know is that the stable is empty, and the horse is gone. The rest I don't know. Whether it be a curse or a blessing, I can't say. All we can see is a fragment. Who can say what will come next?"

The people of the village laughed. They thought that the man was crazy. They had always thought he was a fool; if he wasn't, he would have sold the horse and lived off the money. But instead, he was a poor woodcutter, an old man still cutting firewood and dragging it out of the forest and selling it. He lived hand-to-mouth in the misery of poverty. Now he had proven that he was, indeed, a fool.

After fifteen days, the horse returned. He hadn't been stolen; he had run away into the forest. Not

31

only had he returned, he had brought a dozen wild horses with him. Once again the village people gathered around the woodcutter and spoke. "Old man, you were right and we were wrong. What we thought was a curse was a blessing. Please forgive us."

The man responded, "Once again, you go too far. Say only that the horse is back. State only that a dozen horses returned with him, but don't judge. How do you know if this is a blessing or not? You see only a fragment. Unless you know the whole story, how can you judge? You read only one page of a book. Can you judge the whole book? You read only one word of a phrase. Can you understand the entire phrase? Life is so vast, yet you judge all of life with one page or one word. All you have is a fragment! Don't say that this is a blessing. No one knows. I am content with what I know. I am not perturbed by what I don't."

"Maybe the old man is right," they said to one another. So they said little. But down deep, they knew he was wrong. They knew it was a blessing. Twelve wild horses had returned with one horse. With a little bit of work, the animals could be broken and trained and sold for much money.

The old man had a son, an only son. The young man began to break the wild horses. After a few days, he fell from one of the horses and broke both legs. Once again the villagers gathered around the old man and cast their judgments.

"You were right," they said. "You proved you were right. The dozen horses were not a blessing. They were a curse. Your only son has broken his legs, and now in your old age you have no one to help you. Now you are poorer than ever."

The old man spoke again. "You people are obsessed with judging. Don't go so far. Say only that my son broke his legs. Who knows if it is a blessing or a curse? No one knows. We only have a fragment. Life comes in fragments."

It so happened that a few weeks later the country engaged in war against a neighboring country. All the young men of the village were required to join the army. Only the son of the old man was excluded, because he was injured. Once again the people gathered around the old man, crying and screaming because their sons had been taken. There was little chance that they would return. The enemy was strong, and the war would be a losing struggle. They would never see their sons again.

"You were right, old man," they wept. "God knows you were right. This proves it. Yours son's accident was a blessing. His legs may be broken, but at least he is with you. Our sons are gone forever."

The old man spoke again. "It is impossible to talk with you. You always draw conclusions. No one knows. Say only this: Your sons had to go to war, and mine did not. No one knows if it is a blessing or a curse. No one is wise enough to know. Only God knows."[24]

The old fable points to the fact that it was premature for Naomi to jump to the conclusion that her apparent emptiness, affliction, and misfortune was a curse from God.

A similar situation occurred for a single guy by the name of Joseph in the book of Genesis.[25] Joseph was despised by his brothers who sold him into slavery. As a slave he was falsely charged for a rape that he did not commit. During his resulting imprisonment, for a crime he had not committed, he helped another prisoner achieve his freedom. He was soon forgotten by the man, even when that man was in a position to have helped Joseph gain his freedom. All this sounds like a curse but when he was finally sprung from prison he was elevated to second in command of Egypt. Later, when circumstance grew terrible for his brothers (through, of all things, a "famine in the land"—Genesis 43:1), his brothers came to him for help—but they did not recognize Joseph. When Joseph finally confronted his brothers, who had sold him into slavery out of their jealousy and hatred for him, he said: "You intended to harm me, but God intended it for good to accomplish what is now being done, the saving of many lives" (Genesis 50:20). What had seemed like a curse in the end had become a huge blessing.

The point is, "curse or blessing?" Only time would tell. That was true for Naomi and that is still true today. In fact, the New Testament goes beyond that when it says: "And we know that in all things God works for the good of those who love him, who have been called according to His purpose" (Romans 8:28). Curse or blessing? In the end, according to the book of Romans, it will be a blessing for those who love God and who are called by Him.

Was the divorce or the death a curse? It sure seems so...but God is in the business of overruling that pain with future blessing.

Is living single again a curse or blessing? Only time will tell! Was the divorce or death a curse? It sure seems so, as the single-again person experiences the pain of the recent tragedy—but God is in the business of overruling that pain with future blessing. So time will tell.

The first chapter of this case study closes with this conclusion:

1:22 So Naomi returned from Moab accompanied by Ruth the Moabitess, her daughter-in-law, arriving in Bethlehem as the barley harvest was beginning.

You might say Naomi went home bitter, while Ruth went on to get better. As we will see, even going home bitter is better than turning back on God for the old life, as Orpah did.

Any Time is the Right Time to Return

Now, the timing of Naomi and Ruth's arrival was perfect. It was harvest time. That meant it was time for the "Feast of Firstfruits." There were two feasts that acted like bookends to the harvest season. One was the Feast of Firstfruits which came at the very beginning of the barley season.[26] It denoted that prosperity was on the way, more crops were coming, or more pointedly, "you are about to experience the blessing of God." In a certain sense, it showed that the old was gone and the new was about to come. Now the other bookend to the harvest was the "Feast of Ingathering."[27] It came at the close of the harvest with a celebration of thanksgiving for all the bounty God had bestowed.

Ruth and Naomi arrived at the beginning of harvest. That meant there was food and that plenty more was coming. You might say that God was now working the bad times into good ones. They were about to reap the blessing of others' labor. Others had sown seed in Bethlehem and God blessed them with a rainy season that brought about the germination of the seed. God shined down from heaven His sunlight to bring growth to the seed, and now it was time to harvest.

The same was true for these two single-again women. They had sown their lives in Moab and famine took it all. Now they had returned to God's place of blessing, to "the land," to Bethlehem, and the timing was perfect.

35

There is no bad time to return to the place of God's will, no matter how far you have wandered, no matter how much you have lost, and no matter how much crow you have to eat to do so. When you return to the Lord, harvest time begins. You will reap His blessings. Returning won't be easy, but you will be blessed. You will see this is so from the second part of this case study.

Chapter One Notes

¹ The Book of Ruth is named after the main female heroine of the story found in the book. She was a Moabitess who, after becoming single again, migrated to Israel with her single-again mother-in-law. She played an important part in the ancestry of both King David (4:22) and Jesus Christ (Matthew 1:5). Her name in Hebrew means "friendship." Her male counterpart is the hero of the Book of Ruth. His named was "Boaz;" He was a never-married single man. His name in Hebrew means "strength." This case study zeroes in on these two people named "Friendship" and "Strength."

Jewish tradition attributes the authorship of the book to Samuel. However, there is no internal or external evidence to substantiate or refute that tradition.

The date of the book is set forth in the first line of the book. It took place in the period of the Judges which extended from the death of Joshua and the elders and continued until the first monarch of Israel, King Saul—from approximately 1390 B.C. to 1050 B.C. That was around 340 years. By examining the genealogy in 4:21-22, it becomes apparent that there were four generations from Boaz to David. Leon Wood argued effectively that Boaz, the hero of the Book of Ruth, lived at the same time as Gideon. The genealogy in Judges 4:18-22 ends with David's birth. "David was anointed king in 1010 B.C. at the age of thirty (2 Sam. 5:4, 5). This means that he was born in 1040 B.C. Being the youngest of eight sons in his family (1 Sam 16:10, 11), his father Jesse was probably born at least forty years earlier, or not later that 1080 B.C. Correspondingly, Obed, his father, and Boaz, Obed's father and husband of Ruth, would have been prior to this, making the time of Boaz' vigorous life, as manifested in the story, possibly in the vicinity of 1140 B.C. This places him about the middle of the forty-years of peace period, when Gideon served as judge." See Leon Wood, *Distressing Days of the Judges*, Zondervan, 1975, p. 254.

The book itself covers an eleven to twelve year period. The style of the book is that of historical narrative—or storytelling. The purpose of the book appears to have been to focus on the lineage of King David (4:18-22). The genealogy looks back 900 years to Jacob, and looks ahead around 100 years to David's birth. The purpose underscores God's providential care in a romantic story that brought two single people's lives together to advance the line of the Messiah.

2 The Book of the Judges extended from 1390 B.C – 1050 B.C. The Book of Ruth took place somewhere around 1140 B.C. (See Note 1 above).

3 God had promised the land of Canaan to Abraham (Genesis 12) and confirmed that promise with a covenant (Genesis 15). In Genesis 12:7 it says, "The LORD appeared to Abram and said, 'To your offspring I will give this land.'" In Genesis 15:7 He said, "To your descendants I give this land."

4 See Exodus 3:8; 17; 13:5; 33:3 and many more.

5 The promise of inheriting the land was extended to Isaac. In Genesis 26:2-3 it states, "The LORD appeared to Isaac and said, 'Do not go down to Egypt; live in the land where I tell you to live. 3 Stay in this land for a while, and I will be with you and will bless you. For to you and your descendants I will give all these lands and will confirm the oath I swore to your father Abraham.'" Later, Jacob was instructed to leave the land. Genesis 46:3 records, "I am God, the God of your father," he said. "Do not be afraid to go down to Egypt, for I will make you into a great nation there. 4 I will go down to Egypt with you, and I will surely bring you back again." The sojourn to Egypt would last 430 years and then they would return to conquer the land, just as God had predicted in Genesis 15. Genesis 15:13 records, "Then the LORD said to him, 'Know for certain that your descendants will be strangers in a country not their own, and they will be enslaved and mistreated four hundred years. 14 But I will punish the nation they serve as slaves, and afterward they will come out with great possessions.'" The period of Egyptian bondage was followed by the Exodus, wilderness wanderings, and then anticipation on re-entering the land. God promised to

bless those who re-entered the land. Deuteronomy 28:8 and 30:16 put it this way: "The LORD your God will bless you in the land he is giving you," again, "And the LORD your God will bless you in the land you are entering to possess." Most of the focus of the Books of Deuteronomy, Joshua, and Judges is on living in the Promised Land with God's blessing. There is a sense in which to be in the land is to be in the sphere of God's blessing. It's to be in the will of God because that's where God wanted them.

6 The Hebrew word for Bethlehem is a combination of two Hebrew words:" house" בית (*beth*) and "bread" לחם (*lechem*) and means "place of bread" (See BDB p. 111).

7 The Hebrew name "Judah" יהודה means "praised" (See BDB p. 397). This is further substantiated by its first occurrence in Genesis 29:35 where it says, "She conceived again, and when she gave birth to a son she said, 'This time I will praise the LORD.' So she named him Judah."

8 The name "Moab" מואב [alternate form מאב] (*moab*) appears to be a combination of the preposition *m* which means "*from*" and the Hebrew word for "father," *ab*. Together the name means "from father." The *m* (*mo*) may be a paragogic syllable, attached to the *ab*, so as to form an independent word. In such a case, the word "Moab" would appear to mean "father."

9 The Hebrew name "Lot" לוט (*lot*) means "wrap closely, tightly, enwrap, envelope" (BDB p. 532). It is clear from his story in Genesis 19 that God placed him in an envelope of protection from the judgment that befell Sodom and Gomorrah.

10 See Genesis 13:10.

11 Genesis 19:26 "But Lot's wife looked back, and she became a pillar of salt."

12 Genesis 19:32-38

³² Let's get our father to drink wine and then lie with him and preserve our family line through our father."

³³ That night they got their father to drink wine, and the older daughter went in and lay with him. He was not aware of it when she lay down or when she got up.

³⁴ The next day the older daughter said to the younger, "Last night I lay with my father. Let's get him to drink wine again tonight, and you go in and lie with him so we can preserve our family line through our father."

³⁵ So they got their father to drink wine that night also, and the younger daughter went and lay with him. Again he was not aware of it when she lay down or when she got up.

³⁶ So both of Lot's daughters became pregnant by their father.

³⁷ The older daughter had a son, and she named him Moab; he is the father of the Moabites of today.

³⁸ The younger daughter also had a son, and she named him Ben-Ammi; he is the father of the Ammonites of today.

13 The Hebrew name "Elimelech" אלימלך (*elimelech*) is a nominal, declarative sentence. *Eli* is a combination of the word God (*El*) and the possessive suffix "my" (*-i*) and means, "My God." The being verb is understood. The word "king" (*melech*) complements the subject. So the name reads "My God is King."

14 The Hebrew name "Naomi" נעמי (*noomi*) is a combination of the word "pleasantness, beauty, kindness, favor" (*noam*) with a possessive personal pronoun "my" (*-i*) attached. Her name means, "my pleasantness." (See BDB p. 654).

15 The Hebrew name "Mahlon" מחלון (*mahlon*) is from the root חלה which means "sick" (TWOT, vol.1, p. 652).

16 The Hebrew name "Kilion" כליון (*kilion*) means "failing, pining" (BDB p. 479).

17 The Hebrew word "Ephrathites" אפרתים (*'eprathim)* is a plural adjective that denotes those from Ephrathah. Ephrathah was the area occupied by the descendants of Ephraim. Ephraim was the second son of Joseph. His name means "double fruit." (See

TWOT vol. 1, p. 66). Genesis 41:52 confirms this: "The second son he named Ephraim and said, 'It is because God has made me fruitful in the land of my suffering.'"

[18] The Hebrew name עָרְפָּה "Orpah" is a feminine proper noun based on the word עֹרֶף (*oreph*) which means "back of neck" (See BDB, p. 791).

[19] In both the Books of Exodus and Judges, the noun עֹרֶף (*oreph*) was used for the concept of "turn back" or "retreat" in battle (see Exodus 23:37; Joshua 7:8; 7:12).

[20] The expression "stiff-necked" combines the word "stiff" קְשֵׁה (*qasheh*) and the word "neck" עֹרֶף "*orep*" in numerous passages: Exodus 32:9; 33:3, 5; 34:9 and more.

[21] The name "Ruth" רוּת means "friendship" (BDB p. 946).

[22] The name "Marah" מָרָה (*marah*) means "bitterness" (BDB p. 946).

[23] The well-established stages of grief were introduced by Elizabeth Kübler-Ross, in her book *On Death and Dying* (1969). The stages may be summed up like this:

> First Stage: Denial and Isolation: *"No, not me, it cannot be true."*
> Second Stage: Anger: *"Why me? It's not fair."*
> Third Stage: Bargaining: *"Just let me live to see …."*
> Fourth Stage: Depression: *"I'm so sad. Why bother with anything?"*
> Fifth Stage: Acceptance: *"It's going to be OK."*

[24] Although the exact origin of this fable is unknown, the version cited herein was posted on the internet by Max Lucado at: http://www.maxlucado.com/read/woodcutter/index2.html.

[25] The full "Joseph narration" is found in Genesis 30-50.

[26] The Barley Harvest began in the spring (around April) and lasted from four to six weeks. The beginning of the barley harvest

marked the Feast of First Fruits (Leviticus 23:10). The barley harvest was followed by the wheat harvest.

27 The Feast of Booths was the last feast of the calendar year and was celebrated in September/October. Besides the construction of the booths, other festivities included the ingathering of the labor of the field (Exodus 23:16), the ingathering of the threshing floor and winepress (Deuteronomy 16:13), and the ingathering of the fruit of the earth (Leviticus 23:39).

Part Two:
"Lord, What Do Godly Single Woman Want?"

God the Holy Spirit is actually the Case Worker behind the recording of this study.[1] He deliberately interrupted this case study at the first verse of chapter two in order to make an important insertion. Most people miss this interruption, but it's there. The key to detecting this insertion is to read the last verse of chapter one, skip the first verse of chapter two, and go on to the second verse of chapter two. The case study reads without missing a beat. Read it for yourself:

> **1:22 So Naomi returned from Moab accompanied by Ruth the Moabitess, her daughter-in-law, arriving in Bethlehem as the barley harvest was beginning.**
> ↓ **[Skip 2:1 Now Naomi had a relative on her husband's side, from the clan of Elimelech, a man of standing, whose name was Boaz.]**
> **2:2 And Ruth the Moabitess said to Naomi, "Let me go to the fields and pick up the leftover grain behind anyone in whose eyes I find favor." Naomi said to her, "Go ahead, my daughter."**

So what is so significant about chapter two and verse one that the Holy Spirit interrupted the narrative to insert it? Well, tucked away in that first verse of chapter two is an extraordinary truth for us, the readers. So what is the truth?

It's not that there was a man who's "name was Boaz." The name "Boaz" will be mentioned just four sentences later in verse 3. So there was hardly a need to interrupt the case study to tell us his name. It will surface soon enough. Neither did the Divine Case Worker interrupt the study to tell us that Naomi had a husband; we already knew that from chapter 1:2. Nor was it that "Naomi had a relative on her husband's side," because later, in this same chapter (2:20), Boaz will be called a "kinsman-redeemer." Now a "kinsman-redeemer" could only be a relative from the husband's side (Deuteronomy 25:5), as we will notice in more detail later. No, the reason the Holy Spirit interrupted this case study was to tell us that this man, Boaz, was a "man of standing"[2] (as rendered by the New International Version [NIV]). But the NIV's rendering is not the most suitable. A much better rendering would be "a mighty man of valor." That's how it was rendered in the King James Version of the Bible in the book of the Judges.[3] Now that's what the Divine Case Worker wanted the readers of this case study to know—Boaz was a "mighty man of valor!" He was a strong man. This is so important that He interrupted the case study to let us in on this little secret that at least one person in the narrative (Ruth) did not yet know.

Godly Women Want A Strong Man

So the question that needs to be asked is: "What is so important about being a "mighty man of valor" that the Case Worker would interrupt the narrative?" It appears that the Case Worker did so to reveal that God knew the kind of man Ruth wanted before *she* knew what she wanted. She wanted a "mighty man of valor" like Boaz. Nothing has changed since then. The truth is that even now *every single godly*

> The truth is that even now *every single godly woman wants a mighty man of valor!* She wants a "strong man."

woman wants a mighty man of valor! She wants a "strong man."

Now, this may be a little intimidating to the male reader. You see this short phrase "mighty man of valor" conjures up for the male all sorts of body building images, such as Arnold Schwarzenegger in Conan the Barbarian (or some other power body builder). When the average guy compares himself to that kind of image he feels inadequate. "If that's what a godly woman wants—it's sure not me," he retorts. You see, men focus on the one word "mighty" in that phrase. They immediately assign to it the concept of "physical strength," "courageous power," or "bravery." But women focus on the second part of the phrase. They focus on the word "valor." They want a mighty man of *"VALOR!"* –a man strong in character! Now, if he turns out to be physically strong, handsome, powerful, and courageous, well, that would be viewed as a bonus.

What a godly woman wants is something much deeper than outward appearance. Even though the phrase "mighty man of valor" could mean the external physical condition, [9] and in some instances it did, it is very interesting that the very first time this expression was used in the Biblical record, it was used of a coward named "Gideon" (a contemporary of Boaz).

Gideon, in Judges 6, was trying to hide his crop from the invading Midianites army that had been terrorizing his country for years. He was not a heroic figure who planned to take on the enemy. No, instead of contesting them out of bravery, he rather sheepishly tried to sneak his harvest by the Midianites. He hoped that they wouldn't catch him and take it away. Instead of bravely threshing his crops at the threshing floor, he was threshing his crop secretly in a wine vat. That was the last place he expected that the Midianite terrorists would have looked to plunder his harvest.

It was while he was trying to sneak his harvest past the terrorists that God appeared to him and said to him, "The LORD is with you, mighty man of valor" (Judges 6:12). Notice that God called him a "mighty man of valor."

Gideon, however, did not view himself as such. He protested, "My clan is the weakest in Manasseh, and I am the least in my family" (Judges 6:15). What Gideon was really saying was, "Lord, you've got the wrong guy!"

Now, not only did Gideon not feel like a mighty man of valor, his life was not characterized by one either. He had no desire to perform macho exploits of deliverance. He was a coward who acted accordingly. His life's story was one of overcoming his cowardice. The fact is that when God told Gideon to knock down his father's family idol—he did so, but only at night, for fear of being identified (Judges 6:27). Next, God told Gideon to engage the Midianites in battle and Gideon's first move was to try and weasel his way out of doing that as well. He tried to manipulate God's clearly revealed will for his life with a fleece throwing shenanigan.[4] First, he said to God:

> If you will save Israel by my hand as you have promised—look, I will place a wool fleece on the threshing floor. If there is dew only on the fleece and all the ground is dry, then I will know that you will save Israel by my hand, as you said. (Judges 6:36, 37)

Gideon actually acknowledged that God promised to "save Israel by his hand." He knew what God's will for his life was. God had clearly told him. So Gideon was really just a coward who was attempting to get out of the job that he knew God had called him to do!

Isn't it just like God to accommodate our stubborn whims and overpower them? Well, God accommodated Gideon's whim and made it dew only on the fleece and not on the ground. But that miraculous sign did not empower Gideon with bravery, nor was he convinced that he was the man for the job! No! He still tried to weasel his way out of God's call. Gideon then said, "This time make the fleece dry and the ground covered with dew." Again, God accommodated his whim. The point of all of this is that Gideon, whom God called a "mighty man of valor," was actually a coward at heart.

His cowardice persisted even when Gideon did as God commanded. God commanded that Gideon summon an army to challenge the Midianite invaders. He did, and 32,000 men were mustered. It was then that God said to Gideon, "You have too many men." God knew if He delivered Israel with such a large army, Israel would have believed that "her own strength has saved her" (Judges 7:2). So God instructed Gideon to tell the men in his army that if any were "afraid," they should go home. To Gideon's chagrin, 22,000 men left. You get the feeling that Gideon would have liked to have left as well. He only had 10,000 men. Oh, did we mention that there were 135,000 experienced terrorists in the Midianite army? (See Judges 8:10)

Next, God spoke to Gideon: "There are still too many men." So God instructed Gideon to sift the army once more. Well, that sifting left Gideon with only 300 men. Consider that number and the number of the enemy. The Midianites had 135,000 experienced terrorists; Israel had 300 farmers and shepherds. That was a ratio of 450 terrorists to one good guy—pretty scary odds. God knew Gideon would be afraid with such odds. So, God said to Gideon, "If you are afraid to attack, go down to the camp … and listen to what they are saying" (Judges 7:10). Well, of course Gideon was afraid—so he went down. When he approached the edge of their camp he heard the Midianite soldiers say with their own mouths that they were more afraid of Gideon than Gideon was of them (Judges 7:9-14). This was God's way of encouraging Gideon.

So what does Gideon have to do with Boaz in our case study? What does Gideon have to do with singleness? Everything! Both Gideon and Boaz lived at the same approximate time and both were called a "mighty man of valor."[5] Furthermore, it was from Gideon's life that we discover that the phrase, "mighty man of valor," did not necessarily have to do with physical power, bravery, or

47

unwavering courage. It had more to do with *trusting God to overcome one's fears* and *acting obediently to God's instructions* to conquer one's fears. That takes strong character.

This concept of strong character is true for other men who were called a "mighty man of valor," as well. The other men included the likes of Judge Jephthah, who was called a "mighty man of valor" in Judges 11:1, and like Jeroboam, who was also called a "mighty man of valor" in 1 Kings 11:28. A Syrian commander named Naaman too was called a "mighty man of valor" in 2 Kings 5:1. Each one had an obstacle to overcome. Jephthah's obstacle was rejection. Jeroboam had to overcome his lower class status. Naaman had to overcome leprosy. Each one, with God's help, overcame the obstacle that life threw at them. Each "mighty man of valor" reached deeply within himself to find the faith that would overcome the obstacle in his path. Each had strong character.

Now what is truly amazing is that the man credited with being physically the mightiest man in the Bible, Samson, was *not* called a "mighty man of valor." He had physical power when the Spirit of God came upon him, but he was not a man of "valor." Samson's character was suspect on every side. You see, the idea of being a "mighty man of valor" has more to do with internal integrity than with external strength—Samson was short on the internal. He was a very carnal, worldly man. God used him, but only in spite of Samson, not because Samson was a man of integrity.

You see, what *every* single godly woman wants is a man strong on the inside. Strong enough to share his emotions; strong enough to humble himself and rely on God instead of himself.

The men who feel a little intimidated by the idea that what every single godly woman wants is a "mighty man of valor," should realize that it is not about physical strength. It's not even about power, influence, wealth, or looks—it's about character to overcome the obstacles of life by trusting God. You see, what *every* single godly woman wants is a man strong on the inside. Strong enough to share his emotion. Strong enough to share his fears, weaknesses, and concerns. Strong enough to open up and reveal what's going on inside. Strong enough to humble himself and rely on God instead of himself. It's about internal character that obeys God, no matter what. Obedience that will overcome an external famine such as the famine that struck Israel. Elimelech didn't have it—he fled from hardship.

That's what brings us back to our case study at chapter two, verse one. This "mighty man of valor," who was named "Boaz," stuck it out through the famine. He came out on the other side of the famine better than before. Another interesting feature about Boaz is that his name "Boaz" means "Strength."[6] What a contrast to Mahlon (sickly) and Kilion (pining). Both died during the famine. The fact that Boaz (the strong one) is called a "mighty man of valor" indicates that he was not just strong in name but strong in character as well. He is the opposite of Elimelech whose name meant "My God is King," but whose character was really that of a hypocrite. In reality God was not Elimelech's king at all. But Boaz was, in fact, a strong, mighty man of valor.

Men, ask yourself, "Am I a Boaz or an Elimelech? Am I a strong man of character or a hypocrite? Am I a Boaz or a Mahlon and Kilion. Am I a strong man or a weak, sickly, pining-away kind of person? The reason that the Divine Case Worker interrupted this case study was to reveal the first of several characteristics that every single godly woman wants. She wants a "mighty man of *valor*." The interruption tells us that Boaz was exactly what Ruth wanted, but she didn't know it yet!

"Does God know what I want before I do...?" Of course He does. So you need to get close to God to find out what God wants for you.

The point is, God knew what Ruth wanted before she did. It's also true that God knew what Boaz wanted before he knew it, too. So ask yourself, "Does God know what I want before I do as well?" Of course He does. So you need to get close to God to find out what God wants for you. Then you must trust Him for that someone. Will you do that, or will you take matters into your own hands and settle for a weak pining away relationship?

Adjusting to the Single Life

The second verse of the second chapter resumes with Naomi and Ruth facing the hard realities of living single again. They had to *make some tough adjustments* to the new single life in a different environment. Of course there was the whole issue of finding work. This is not as hard for some people as others. For me, moving on was tough—the church had let me go, due to the impending divorce. Finding a job, just to have a positive cash flow, meant working any available job. I started with the temp agency, Manpower, doing mundane, minimum-wage, entry-level, factory work. On top of all my pain from the divorce, I felt so humiliated. Fallen from a respected Senior Pastor position to working mostly with high school students for minimum wage. I moved from that temporary position to a part-time night job at Airborne Express as a package sorter. Then I picked up another part-time day job at a retail store. I worked both at the same time; one part-time job during the day and another part-time job at night. Now when you lose it all, you take whatever is available. Not every person living single again finds himself or herself experiencing such humiliating circumstances. Still, some experience even worse. Ruth did. The case study says:

2:2 ...Ruth the Moabitess said to Naomi, "Let me go to the fields and pick up the leftover grain behind anyone in whose eyes I find favor." Naomi said to her, "Go ahead, my daughter."

Godly Women Want to be Noticed

God's law of the land stated that the harvesters could not harvest every bit of the crops. They could not make a second pass, nor could they harvest the corners of the fields. The corners and missed harvest was to be left for those in need—for the poor and destitute (Leviticus 19:9,10). Ruth volunteered to publicly lower herself and join the destitute beggars who followed the paid harvesters in order to collect the leftovers, just to survive. The process of collecting "leftovers" was called "gleaning." It was her hope that she would find favor in the eyes of some landowner who would allow a foreigner like herself to glean in his fields. You might say that she wanted to be noticed favorably. Godly women still do.

There is no telling all the various humbling avenues readers have pursued in the course of trying to bring some stability back to their lives. Some readers may still be in the humiliating experience, and still others may have yet to go through deeply humiliating circumstances just to survive. At desperate times you will need a plan of action and then need to act on that plan. That's exactly what Ruth did next:

2:3 So she went out and began to glean in the fields behind the harvesters. As it turned out, she found herself working in a field belonging to Boaz, who was from the clan of Elimelech.

The case study says, "As it turned out." You see, Ruth had no idea that what she and others perceived as a random, chance event was actually a divinely appointed event. It was no mistake that she "found herself working in a field belonging to Boaz." God had providentially orchestrated her plan to achieve His goal. God did so to place her where He wanted her to be. He had used every circumstance in her entire life to bring her to that field on that day. The point here is that before we ever make our plans, God has already

This should give us all hope. As we face today it may be just another routine ordinary day, but God may be assigning to it a life-defining moment. providentially orchestrated our plans as part of His master plan. He does so to achieve the goal of His greater master plan. Like Ruth, we never know what a day will bring forth. Only time will tell. Often only hindsight will tell what the defining moments of any day were. Let's face it, on the day that Ruth chose to go to the field it was just another uncertain day—but looking back on the day, in the full scope of her life, it was an extra-ordinary day.

This should give us all hope. As we face today it may be just another routine ordinary day, but God may be assigning to it a life-defining moment. We will not know until a future time when we can look back on today and see how God orchestrated it in the master plan. Here's how her day unfolded....

2:4 While she was there, Boaz arrived from Bethlehem and greeted the harvesters. "The LORD be with you!" he said. "The LORD bless you!" the harvesters replied. 5 Then Boaz asked his foreman, "Who is that girl over there?" 6 And the foreman replied, "She is the young woman from Moab who came back with Naomi. 7 She asked me this morning if she could gather grain behind the harvesters. She has been hard at work ever since, except for a few minutes' rest over there in the shelter." (NLT)

Godly Women Want a Relationship That Will Last

In the Living Single Again DVD video series[7] that I developed as a post divorce recovery group study, I laid out the 12 Steps to bonding a relationship for life (See chart 1).

```
┌─────────────────────────────────────────────────────────┐
│  ┌──────────────────┐      GENITAL TO GENITAL  │ 12      │
│  │    Chart 1:      │                                     │
│  │  The 12 Steps    │      HAND TO GENITAL   │ 11         │
│  │  to Bonding a    │                                     │
│  │Relationship for Life│   MOUTH TO BREAST   │ 10         │
│  └──────────────────┘                                     │
│                        HAND TO BODY  │ 9                  │
│                     HAND TO HEAD  │ 8                     │
│                 MOUTH TO MOUTH  │ 7                        │
│                   6 │ ARM TO WAIST                        │
│                 5 │ ARM TO SHOULDER                       │
│               4 │ HAND TO HAND                            │
│             3 │ VOICE TO VOICE   ┌─────────────────────┐  │
│           2 │ EYE TO EYE         │  An adaptation from │  │
│                                  │    Donald Joy,      │  │
│         1 │ EYE TO BODY          │     Bonding,        │  │
│                                  │     p.43-53.        │  │
│                                  └─────────────────────┘  │
└─────────────────────────────────────────────────────────┘
```

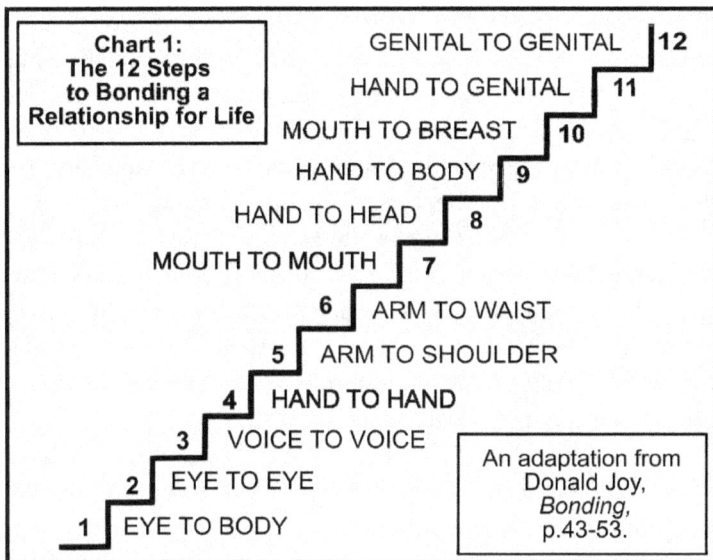

These steps were first developed by Desmond Morris in his book *Intimate Behaviors*[8] and have been followed by Christian writers such as Donald Joy in his book *Bonding*[9] and Norman Wright in his book *Relationships that Work and Those that Don't*.[10] Without attempting to superimpose these 12 Steps on the Bible, I would like to note how some of the steps surface in this case study of Ruth and Boaz.

According to the fourth verse, when "Boaz arrived ... Boaz asked... "Who is that girl over there?" (NLT) Boaz took notice of Ruth. I would like to suggest that his "taking notice of her" follows the First Step of the 12 Steps of bonding a relationship for life. He didn't know it, but he took the first step.

The First Step is called "Eye to Body" because it involves taking notice of a person of the opposite sex and asking oneself something like, "Where have you been all my life?" Boaz did more than ask himself. He blurted it out loud to his field foreman. Boaz noticed Ruth and being noticed was what Ruth had wanted from the start (see Ruth 2:2).

This case study reveals some of the 12 Steps, but does so out of order. Step 3 of the 12 Steps to bonding a relationship for life is called "Voice to Voice" and it appears in the text before Step 2, "Eye to Eye." The Second Step, "Eye to Eye," involves the discovery that while one is checking out the other, the other is checking out the original looker too. Somehow, in an almost enchanting way the eyes of both look into the others eyes. Suddenly, a rush of embarrassment flushes both their faces as they have both been caught gazing intently into each other's eyes. The case study does not give us graphic details of this encounter as it seemingly skips it to get on to Step 3, the "Voice to Voice" step.

Step 3 is called "Voice to Voice" because each asks, "What will I say to this person for the first time?" "How will I respond if they talk to me?" "Will I say something acceptable or stupid?" You see, each has talked to hundreds of people of the opposite sex before—but this is different because each wants to make a good impression on the other. As we read between the lines, we may safely assume that Boaz thinks within himself, "How am I going to introduce myself to her in a way that she notices me." His "voice to voice" encounter went like this ...

2:8 So Boaz said to Ruth, "My daughter, listen to me. Don't go and glean in another field and don't go away from here. Stay here with my servant girls. 9 Watch the field where the men are harvesting, and follow along after the girls. I have told the men not to touch you. And whenever you are thirsty, go and get a drink from the water jars the men have filled."

Pretty smooth. Boaz has suppressed his initial inquisitive forwardness that he blurted out to the foreman. He masked his piqued curiosity by taking the "less-interested" approach. He appealed to her from a more elderly or fatherly perspective. He called her "my daughter." This expression is, of course, an endearing one. Implied within it is the idea of family relationship. But it also indicated something more. Namely, that she was, in fact, much younger than he was. He did not let her in on his intrigue with her. Nevertheless, he did invite her to stay, offered her a status with his servants (a step up from beggar), offered protection, and suggested she take an occasional break to get a drink. Boaz was acting very much like people in our culture—a little protective of his true feelings. He was not letting her in on his true feelings all at once. He wanted to place himself in the best light. He may have even quickly assessed that he was too old to be a serious contender for the interest of a younger woman like Ruth, but already knew that he would like her company. As within our culture, when dating begins, both people attempt to portray themselves in their best light—so Boaz appears to have done the same.

Ruth's voice to voice response indicated that she was aware that Boaz had noticed her in a significant way....

2:10 At this, she bowed down with her face to the ground. She exclaimed, "Why have I found such favor in your eyes that you notice me—a foreigner?"

From the beginning Ruth desired to be noticed by someone who would allow her to glean (2:1), and now in fact, she had been noticed. Her initial desire to be noticed was not in any other way than to be afforded the opportunity to glean in a field; but it is obvious that Boaz noticed her in a more significant way. Well, this noticing one another parallels the Second Step of "Eye to Eye." They had, in all likelihood, had an eye-to-eye encounter before, or at least with that first conversation.

Boaz continued with more of Step 3: "Voice to Voice:"

2:11 ...Boaz replied. "But I also know about the love and kindness you have shown your mother-in-law since the death of your husband. I have heard how you left your father and mother and your own land to live here

among complete strangers. (NLT)

Ruth, no doubt, was the talk of the town—but in a good way. Even Boaz had heard of her. He was so impressed by her leaving Moab for Bethlehem that he blessed her...

2:12 "May the LORD repay you for what you have done. May you be richly rewarded by the LORD, the God of Israel, under whose wings you have come to take refuge."

Boaz was such a man of valor. He did not hesitate to bring up the LORD with her. He was not afraid to talk about God and his faith. Since blessings are a form of prayer in which the person praying invokes God to be favorable toward another person, you might say, he prayed for her. He did this because he had learned of her conversion experience. This is the stuff that a godly woman wants from a mighty man of valor—a man who will openly discuss the Lord, his faith, and even pray with her.

> **This is the stuff that a godly woman wants from a mighty man of valor--a man who will openly discuss the Lord, his faith, and even pray.**

Ruth responded to Boaz with a little more of Step 3: "Voice to Voice" talk. She appealed to his eyes and so much more:

2:13 "May I continue to find favor in your eyes, my lord," she said. "You have given me comfort and have spoken kindly to your servant—though I do not have the standing of one of your servant girls."

Godly Women Want Four Qualities in a Man

Ruth made a request of Boaz. In her request were the

seeds of four qualities that every single godly woman desires of a man of valor. When these seeds are watered in a relationship, they can grow to fulfill a woman's deepest desires.

The first seed planted was a desire for the attention of a man of valor. As relationships grow, women desire undivided attention—eyes only for her. At this point, Ruth would be happy to just have continued attention through the harvest season so she could make a living for herself and Naomi.

Second, every single godly woman wants to be favored by a man of valor. The word "favor" literally means "graced."[11] It possesses the idea of receiving unmerited, undeserved, and unconditional favor—being accepted without jumping through a series of hoops to earn that acceptance.

Third, every single godly woman wants to receive comfort from a man of valor. This assumes that he sees beyond himself. It assumes that he sees the emotional pain of others. It also assumes that he can verbally console her.

The last of the seeds planted regarding what every single godly woman wants is a simple communication called "conversation." Not just any conversation—but deep conversation—that touches the heart. When Ruth said to Boaz, "you have spoken kindly," the case study literally says that he had "spoken to (or from) the heart."[12] He was a man in touch with his feelings and a man who could express them verbally, in such a way that her heart was touched by him. All this was revealed in a brief conversation that took place at Step 3, on the first day they met.

Steps 1-3 often go by very quickly. They did for Boaz and Ruth. They did for me as well. I had been asked to be part of a panel discussion for a singles group at another church. The topic was, "Singles and Sexuality" and the audience could ask any question they desired. I don't know why I accepted the invitation to be part of that panel discussion, but I did. All the way to the meeting that evening

I kept asking myself why I had allowed myself to be part of the panel. I deliberately arrived early so I could greet everyone as they arrived (I always feel more comfortable speaking to a group when I am acquainted with them). So I endeavored to greet each of the hundred or so singles who arrived at the meeting, just to have a feel for my audience. During the panel discussion I noticed a rather attractive woman who arrived and that I had not previously met. My first response was "Wow, how had I missed her?" "How can I meet her?"

Well, as I was on the panel, I couldn't help myself from glancing constantly in her direction. Suddenly, I realized she was gazing back at me the same way I was at her. Somehow we both knew it. We had caught each other staring into the eyes of each other with a bit of embarrassment. We both glanced away.

After the meeting, I positioned myself at the door to chat with each person as they were exiting and, of course, so I could talk to the attractive woman with whom I made eye contact. It happened. She approached the door and I had to say something, for the first time, directly to her. After some pleasantries, I learned where she worked and told her I worked less than a mile from where she did. I then added, "I'll stop by your work and see you sometime." Well, two days later, I did. (Later we married each other.) However, in just a few moments of interaction, Dianne and I, just like Boaz and Ruth, were at Step 3. It does not go this quickly for all couples. Often one will have interest piqued while the other doesn't even notice. Donald Joy says, "If the discovery is one-sided, there may be long days, or months of gazing without the return of the magic look."[13]

Godly Women Want Someone with Whom to Share

The next three stages of bonding a relationship for life are Step 4: "Hand to Hand;" Step 5: "Arm to Shoulder;" and, Step 6: "Arm to Waist." One of the things that each has in common is "physical touch." It is rather obvious that the concept of dating, as we know, is foreign to Bible times. Their courtship was not as physical as it is in our lives. Still, they had a culturally acceptable process of courting that accomplished the same thing as our process. For example, all three steps (4-6) are social statements, in progressive degrees, that say, "We're together." The holding of hands that takes place at Step 4 is the first stage of publicly stating "we're connected." "We're together." The "Arm to Shoulder" gesture of Step 5 is a statement that the two are closer than just acquaintances and the "Arm to Waist" gesture of Step 6 shows they are even more intimate friends. Note what each of these steps have in common is the couple is positioned side-by-side. As such, they view the world together. All the while they talk and share their world views to see if each is compatible with the other before progressing any further in the relationship. This is done without looking into each other's eyes, but looking together in the direction of the world.

Now it appears that, though not formally called a "date," the two named, "Friendship" and "Strength" (Ruth and Boaz), came together in a causal way, similar to a "lunch date."

"Friendship" and "Strength" came together in a causal way, similar to a "lunch date."

2:14 At mealtime Boaz said to her, "Come over here. Have some bread and dip it in the wine vinegar." When she sat down with the harvesters, he offered her some roasted grain. She ate all she wanted and had some left over.

Notice Boaz is the initiator who makes all his "moves" publicly, in a group setting. Boaz' invitation to "Come over here" is a request to be close in proximity. He did not say, "Go sit over there." But "Come over here." He wanted to be with her. Together. Not together alone—but together in a group. Now the case study notices in detail that he treated her in a special way. She sat with him and the harvesters (not with the rest of the gleaners). He offered "her" roasted grain—something the case study does not say he did for the others. And he lavished it on her. The point of all this was that he was publicly saying, "I have an interest in her more than the others."

The nearest the text comes to stating that any physical contact may have occurred is found in the expression "he offered her some roasted grain."[14] This expression may imply that Boaz touched her hand or arm in the process. He may have done so, just as one places one hand under the hand of another person's hand to steady it when attempting to pour or heap something into it. If so, this is the first physical contact.

The first time I held my wife's hand was a month after I had met her. When I took her by the hand as I was driving and she was in the passenger seat of the car, she felt a bit strange. She had only viewed us as friends. She thought I would be just another guy-friend. But holding hands heightened the stakes in the blossoming relationship. It meant we were together. There is power in touch.

Boaz' interest became even more obvious with each remark that he made ...

2:15 As she got up to glean, Boaz gave orders to his men, "Even if she gathers among the sheaves, don't embarrass her. 16 Rather, pull out some stalks for her from the bundles and leave them for her to pick up, and don't rebuke her."

Boaz was protecting her. He was looking out for her. Even though his actions were gestures of generosity, by this time of the day all the harvesters had to be aware that Boaz had a special interest in Ruth. We, the readers of the case study, can tell just from a casual reading of the verse. Of course, "protection" and "provision" are two more qualities that every single godly woman desires. Boaz was doing a good job of both.

After lunch it was time for everyone to return to the fields …

2:17 So Ruth gleaned in the field until evening. Then she threshed the barley she had gathered, and it amounted to about an ephah. 18 **She carried it back to town, and her mother-in-law saw how much she had gathered. Ruth also brought out and gave her what she had left over after she had eaten enough.**

Thanks to Boaz, she had an extra-ordinary harvest from a single day in the field—or, should we say, thanks to the providence of God.   It was God's providential hand that steered her to his field.

Godly Women Want Someone Who Cares

Ruth was in a care group of just two, Naomi and herself. In typical female fashion, that requires an update on all activities of a loved one's day, Naomi needed to know in detail about all that had happened to Ruth that first day in the fields. That "need to know" brought on a barrage of mother-in-law questions …

2:19 Her mother-in-law asked her, "Where did you glean today? Where did you work? Blessed be the man who took notice of you!"

No doubt the quantity of Ruth's gleanings brought about the exclamation of blessing upon the man who noticed Ruth and allowed Ruth to glean in his fields.   At this point, Naomi hadn't learned who he was, but she did know the day had started with hope that Ruth would be noticed by someone—and noticed she was. In response …

2:19 ... Ruth told her mother-in-law about the one at whose place she had been working. "The name of the man I worked with today is Boaz," she said. 20 "The LORD bless him!" Naomi said to her daughter-in-law. "He has not stopped showing his kindness to the living and the dead." She added, "That man is our close relative; he is one of our kinsman-redeemers."

Naomi saw the LORD in all that took place. She knew it was providential, not accidental. She had come back to the land (to God's will) and to the House of Bread as a bitter woman—but now she was blessing others in the name of the LORD again. How quickly her attitude had changed. How quickly she acknowledged the kindness of God. You see, when we do what is right (like returning to God's will), in spite of how we feel (even if we're bitter), our feelings will soon catch up with our doings—feeling good for doing good.

It even went beyond feeling "good" to feeling incredibly awesome. Boaz was their kinsman-redeemer. That meant he was a close relative who, according to Mosaic Law, could do something about their dire situation. Because Ruth was a Moabitess, it is safe to assume she was not an expert on Hebrew Law and that she did not know all the implications of a kinsman-redeemer. But Naomi did. The fact that she did would manifest itself later; but for now the case study resumes with keeping the significance of a kinsman-redeemer under wraps so Ruth could share the rest of what had happened on her first day in the field:

2:21 Then Ruth the Moabitess said, "He even said to me, 'Stay with my workers until they finish harvesting all my grain.'"

This was like saying, "I got the job!" It meant steady income. The cupboards would not be bare. "We've got a future!"

2:22 Naomi said to Ruth her daughter-in-law, "It will be good for you, my daughter, to go with his girls, because in someone else's field you might be harmed." 23 So Ruth stayed close to the servant girls of Boaz to glean until the barley and wheat harvests were finished. And she lived with her mother-in-law.

Boaz' invitation to Ruth to stay on in his fields seems to indicate that he had continued interest in her. It appears safe to say that each had an interest in the other. Boaz was intrigued by her; Ruth found safety and protection in him. The barley and wheat season lasted from around the beginning of our month of March and ended at the end of our month of June or around 120 days. Although they did not date in the typical western style of going out together, it is safe to assume that they did see each other in the larger group setting of working in the fields on a regular basis. They did so for the entire harvest season.

For months Ruth returned to Boaz' field six days a week. Can you imagine how each must have studied the other's characteristics from a distance? You might say that their friendship was progressing slowly—and safely. Unfortunately, in our culture everyone is in a hurry. We demand everything in an instant. When it comes to relationships, the reckless couple hurries through the steps of bonding for life—but not Boaz and Ruth. We can learn from them that friendship takes time to progress.

Though the case study does not tell us how often Boaz frequented his harvesters. With his curiosity piqued as it was, he probably checked in frequently. But because Boaz was a much older single, he may have discounted himself as a serious contender for the heart of this younger single-again woman.

We will see in the next chapter that taking godly advice has a strange way of changing everything—for the good.

Chapter Two Notes

[1] There is no disrespect intended by calling the Holy Spirit of God a Case Worker. In fact, the New Testament calls Him a Counselor (John 14:16, 26; 15:26; 16:7). In our culture, a counselor is often assigned a case and then is called a Case Worker. It is clear that behind the human author, whoever that may have been (see Chapter One Notes, note 1), the ultimate author is God the Holy Spirit. God the Holy Spirit superintended the writing of this Book of the Bible. By that it is meant that God the Holy Spirit "carried along" the human author (2 Peter 1:21). So the actual text that the human author wrote, in its original form, is the "inspired, God-breathed," Word of God (2 Timothy 3:16).

[2] The expression "man of standing" in Hebrew is איש גבור חיל *('ish gibbor khayil)*, literally, a "man mighty strong." Although the words have several possible meanings, "Approximately eighty-five times *hayil* is used as an attribute of people. It follows *'ish* "man" (valiant man," 1 Kgs 1:42), sometimes *ben* "son" ("valiant man," II Sam 17:10), and most often follows *gibbor* "mighty man of valor")…. When the term is used of a woman (Ruth 3:11; Prov 12:4; and 31:10) it is translated "virtuous" (ASV, RSV, "worthy" or "good"), but it may be that a woman of this caliber had all the attributes of her male counterpart." TWOT, vol. 1, pp. 271-2.

[3] The expression was translated as "mighty man of valour" in Judges 6:12 with respect to Gideon, who was possibly a contemporary of Boaz (see note 5 below), and it is used in Judges 11:1 with respect to Jephthah, who judged Israel after Boaz. The usage of the expression "mighty man of valour" should be understood the same for each of these usages.

[4] Leon Wood, *Distressing Days of the Judges*, Zondervan 1975 p. 213-214.

Wood called this episode in Gideon's life "Gideon's sin in asking for reassurance." Wood went on to say regarding Gideon, "…he was wrong in asking God for reassurance by means of the test with the fleece." There are three reasons why he was wrong: "1) God's directive had already been given.... 2) It was an improper type of test.... 3) Gideon did not keep his word."

5 Leon Wood, *Distressing Days of the Judges*, Zondervan 1975 p. 254

Wood argued effectively that Boaz lived at the same time as Gideon (See Chapter One, Note 1). Since Boaz lived during the time of Gideon and before the time of Abimelech, both who were called "mighty men of valor," it only makes sense that however the term, "mighty man of valor" was used of Gideon and Abimelech, it was likewise used of Boaz. This further substantiates that the meaning of the term "mighty man of valor" did not mean "wealthy man" or "man of standing" as translated by the King James or the New International versions. It is best rendered "mighty man of valor."

6 The name "Boaz" בעז (*Boaz*) was derived from the Hebrew word that probably meant "strength." (BDB p. 127) An alternate meaning, "fleetness," has been suggested. That "fleetness" is improbable is seen by the use of the name with the two pillars that stood before Solomon's Temple. The one pillar was named Jakin (established) and the other named Boaz (strength). The alternative rendering of "fleetness" does not fit with the immobility of a pillar nor as a parallel name to "established."

7 Dennis Henderson, *Living Single Again*, (a seven-part DVD videos series), Single Initiative, 2005.

The *Living Single Again* DVD series is a post divorce recovery program. While divorce recovery programs focus on healing past emotional and relational wounds, *Living Single Again* focuses on developing future relationships in a Biblical way that will not repeat past failures. *Living Single Again* is available online at: http://www.LivingSingleAgain.com.

8 Desmond Morris, *Intimate Behavior*, New York: Random House, 1971.

[9] Donald Joy, *Bonding Relationships in the Image of God*, Waco Texas: Word Books, 1985.

[10] Norman Wright, *Relationships that Work: (and Those That Don't)*, Ventura, CA: Regal Books, 1998.

[11] The Hebrew word "favor" חֵן (*hen*) means "grace, favor, kindness" (BDB p.336).

[12] The Hebrew phrase is דברת על־לב שפחתך and literally says "you spoke upon (the) heart of your maid servant." The whole idea of the "heart" is missing in most translations, but very present in the text.

[13] Donald Joy, *Bonding*, Word Books, 1985, p. 44.

[14] The phrase "He offered her" ויצבט־לה contains the Hebrew verb צבט which only occurs here in the Old Testament. The meaning of the verb according to BDB is "grasp, hold, and handle" (BDB p. 840). The Arabic rendering of it is "hold firmly, seize" and the Ethiopic rendered it as "grasp firmly." It seems that physical contact may be implied in this "offer" by Boaz.

Part Three:
"Lord, What Do Godly Single Men Want?"

The previous chapter revealed that every single godly woman wants a "mighty man of valor" who has eyes only for her, who unconditionally favors her, who comforts her, who converses with her, who protects her and who provides for her. Boaz was that kind of man. Now in this third part of the case study the focus turns to the kind of woman a godly man wants.

Tucked away, half-way through this third chapter, Boaz testifies of Ruth, with profound admiration, "All my fellow townsmen know that you are a woman of noble character" (Ruth 3:11). I want to suggest, from that statement by Boaz, that the kind of woman every single godly man wants is "a woman of noble character" like Ruth. The NIV uses the expression "woman of noble character" to describe the quality that Ruth possessed. The KJV uses the expression "virtuous woman" to describe her character. Other translations call her, "a woman of excellence" (NAB), "an honorable woman" (NLT), or other positive expressions. All the translations attempt to render the same Hebrew description of her. This Hebrew expression is best rendered "woman of virtue."[1] This expression is very similar to that which the Divine Case Worker interrupted the second chapter to tell us about Boaz (see 2:1). Boaz was called a "man of valor." Both the words "valor" and "virtue" translate the same Hebrew word. The fact that the Divine Case Worker used the same Hebrew word for both is enlightening. Both have the same quality—one in the male gender and one in the female gender. You see, when the term is used with the male gender, it is rendered "mighty man of valor." Now when it is used with the female gender, it is rendered "woman of virtue. But in reality, the terms are the same, and the quality they possess is the same. "Valor" and "Virtue" are the same internal qualities of an over comer.[2] With this in view, an important principle may be stated:

Every single man and woman reading this book is looking for a "person of valor or virtue." So, what if when you find that "person of valor or virtue," they don't find YOU to be one?

Once I was at lunch with two single friends who were, as guys do, checking out every single woman who entered the restaurant who was not wearing a wedding ring. They would sigh as each beautiful woman entered, "Ah, how could I meet her?"

Then the one single guy said to the other, "You know what our problem is?"

"No," said the other, "What's our problem?"

The first single then replied to the second, "We're a couple of fives looking for a couple of tens!"

Of course, we all laughed, but that is so true for too many singles. They are looking for the "man of valor" (a ten) or "woman of virtue" (a ten) but they themselves are not a ten! Here's the point, "What if when you find that 'person of valor or virtue' (a ten), that person doesn't find you to be a person of valor or virtue (a ten)?"

The bottom line is you must focus on *yourself*—not on a relation-ship! Are you a ten in valor or virtue? Be honest! Or are you a five trying to attract a ten?

Since we've already discussed what a man of valor is (in the pre-vious chapter), perhaps the question that needs to be asked is, "What is a Woman of Virtue?" As we examine the third chapter of this case study, we will attempt to draw out the qualities of the woman of virtue that every single godly man is looking for. So let's return to the text and view it from the perspective of what every single godly man wants.

The bottom line is that you must focus on *yourself*— not on a relationship!

Godly Men Want God's Intervention

God's intervention comes in some pretty mysterious ways. We expect it to come with a trumpet fanfare and red carpet. But more often than not, it comes subtly without hype or fanfare. The case study resumes in a curious way. It simply says, "One day..." This is similar to the second chapter where the study said, "As it turned out, she found herself working in a field belonging to Boaz ...." It may have seemed like a random, accidental, pick-of-the-straw, chance happening; but in fact, God was really working behind the scene. In a similar way this chapter starts with what appears to be just another ordinary day, when it says, "One day...." But this would be no ordinary day. As it turns out, this will be a pivotal day in the lives of the three key single people in this study. The point must not be missed that you never know what a day will bring forth.

So...

3:1 One day Naomi her mother-in-law said to her, "My daughter, should I not try to find a home for you, where you will be well provided for? 2 Is not Boaz, with whose

servant girls you have been, a kinsman of ours? Tonight he will be winnowing barley on the threshing floor.

It doesn't take a rocket scientist to figure out what Naomi was doing at this point in the case study. You might say that before there was Neil Warren Clark's "eharmony" there was Naomi's "bharmony" (Bible harmony). Just like God who brought Adam and Eve together, Naomi, was tactfully match-making. In all likelihood, Naomi had noted everything Ruth had said about her continued interactions with Boaz in the field and at lunch each day. Naomi has put together both Boaz' action and the daily reports from Ruth about Boaz. She knows that he had more than a casual interest in Ruth. Naomi had to be thinking that these two are a match. She's thinking what the two of them may not have been thinking (or perhaps what the two of them hoped for but would not bring themselves to talk about out loud).

Godly Men Want to Date With Purpose

As Naomi pondered this, she came up with a strategy on how to get a man. This is important. You go about courtship (dating) either with or without a strategy. When you do so, without a strategy, you are using the "random/accidental" approach. What is meant by this is that you have no target or goal at which you are aiming. Consequently, you have no strategy by which to arrive at the intended destination. Most daters believe that they will know what they want when they find "it." But how can you find "it" when you don't know what "it" is? How can you strategize when you don't have a goal at which to aim?

> **Most daters believe that they will know what they want when they find "it." But how can you find "it" when you don't know what "it" is?**

70

Now it is true that it was God's providence that brought the two into the same field. But once in the field they needed a strategy. When you develop a strategy, you are using what I call the "deliberate/intentional" approach to dating. This "deliberate/intentional" approach was developed thoroughly in the *Living Single Again* DVD video series study.[3] It is called "Purpose Driven" dating. That simply means that the dater has an intentional goal or purpose for dating. The dater knows what he or she wants from a date before ever going out on a date, and that he or she has a strategy to get to that goal.

There are both appropriate goals and inappropriate goals. The non-Christian dater's goal may be simply "to get lucky" or "to score," while the Christian will have an entirely different goal. The bull's eye on the target at which the Christian aims has written on it 1 Corinthians 10:31, "So whether you eat or drink or whatever you do, do it all for the glory of God." Dating falls into the category of "whatever you do." For the Christian, the foremost goal of dating is to please God on every date.

There is so much more you need to determine before you date. "What does God want for me?" What are the absolutes that I want and that I won't fudge on? What are my preferences (things I prefer but am willing to concede on)? The absolutes of God and your absolutes must never be compromised—while the preferences may be. If you wait until you date to figure out what you want in a mate—it will be too late. Infatuation will take you where you do not really want to go.

In a similar way, Naomi told Ruth that she had a goal for her when she asked: "should I not try to find a home for you, where you will be well provided for?" Provision and protection was a huge thing for women back in the days of the Judges. It still is today.

Naomi's strategy started with identifying the kind of man who would fit that bill. In order to broach the subject with Ruth, Naomi asks a rhetorical question. It's rhetorical because Naomi had already told Ruth that Boaz was kin (Ruth 2:20). She asked: "Is not Boaz, with whose servant girls you have been, a kinsman of ours?" Once Naomi put Boaz on the table for discussion, she made her next move in her well thought out strategy. That move had to do with timing. "Tonight he will be winnowing barley on the threshing floor." Her strategy also had a rather bizarre *detailed* plan:

3:3 "Wash and perfume yourself, and put on your best clothes. Then go down to the threshing floor, but don't let him know you are there until he has finished eating and drinking. 4 When he lies down, note the place where he is lying. Then go and uncover his feet and lie down. He will tell you what to do."

Naomi appeared to have thought hard on this and developed a detailed plan. She must have said to herself, "Boaz has only seen Ruth covered in the dirt and debris from gleaning in the fields. He has only seen the side of her as a field laborer, sweating it out in the hot summer sun, and dressed in work clothes. He needs to see the pretty side of Ruth."

Well, of course the harvest was over, and it was time to thresh the crops. That meant Boaz and the other men would be threshing all day and then celebrating in the evening. They would even sleep at the threshing floor with the grain, through the night, to protect it till daylight.

As the wheels spun in Naomi's mind, idea after idea came to her. Her strategy was to place Ruth in the best possible light before Boaz, so he would see her in a new way. Naomi may not have intended to come across as a bossy mother-in-law, but she already had a history of it. Remember how she was bossing both Orpah and Ruth to go back to Moab in the first chapter of this case study. Well, here she goes again, bossing Ruth to carry out Naomi's plan. Naomi orders Ruth to:

1) Wash herself
2) Perfume herself
3) Put on her best clothes
4) Go where Boaz was
5) Conceal herself
6) Note where Boaz was
7) Go to Boaz
8) Uncover Boaz' feet
9) Lie down by Boaz
10) Listen to Boaz.

Naomi has not simply suggested that Ruth take an interest in Boaz, she has laid out the plan. Naomi's repetitive use of imperatives indicates she was not merely suggesting to Ruth, but actually giving her orders. You might say we see Naomi being a little bossy again.

So how does a "Woman of Virtue" respond to her bossy mother-in-law? Well, she listens with respect and says ...

3:5 "I will do whatever you say," Ruth answered. 6 So she went down to the threshing floor and did everything her mother-in-law told her to do.

Ruth responded with humble submission by yielding to the demands of her mother-in-law. She yielded herself to her Naomi's will. Not in word only, she actually carried out the plan of her mother-in-law. She was submissive. Now submission to God is one thing and submission of one woman to another woman is still another thing. But in our culture today, neither one is as explosive as suggesting that a woman submit to her man. That thought causes nearly all women today to cringe. Why? Perhaps women cringe because of an overbearing man in the past, or perhaps from having been brought up under the influence of the modern women's movement. Still, submission was the quality of this virtuous woman, and it still is a quality of virtuous women today. Ruth not only possessed a submissive spirit to Naomi but, as will be seen, to Boaz as well.

3:7 When Boaz had finished eating and drinking and was in good spirits, he went over to lie down at the far end of the grain pile. Ruth approached quietly, uncovered his feet and lay down. 8 In the middle of the night something startled the man, and he turned and discovered a woman lying at his feet.

A Lot of Respect

Her submissive attitude toward Boaz showed up more as "respect" than anything else. She postured herself to respect him. A servant would lie at his master's feet and would be ready for any command of the master. So, when Naomi told Ruth to lie down at Boaz' feet, she told her to go to him in a totally humble, submissive, and respectful way. In fact, the expression, "at his feet" occurs 25 times in the NIV Bible and is always used to show "respect."[4]

> **The most desired quality that every single godly man wants in a woman is the virtue of "RESPECT."**

The most desired quality that every single godly man wants in his woman is the virtue of "RESPECT." Not only do men want this, God demands it of all married women. Ephesians 5:33 says, "The wife must respect her husband." This is not optional—she *must*. It is in fact unconditional. That means it is to be a gracious act on the part of the woman. She is to offer respect as an unearned, unmerited, unconditional, no-strings-attached gift. A wife is to offer it even when he does not deserve it. That is so counter-culture. Yet it is so Biblical.

In our modern feminist culture there does seem to be a double standard. Women expect men to earn respect; and if a man does something undeserving of it, she has every right to withhold it. At the same time, women do not expect to have to earn his love. Why? Well, women expect men to love them unconditionally, even when they are unlovely. And rightfully so, as Ephesians 5:33 says, regarding men, "each one of you also must love his wife as he loves himself." However, some women believe that men "must" rightly love unconditionally; but, for some mysterious reason, do not feel that they should unconditionally respect their husbands as the Bible says for them to do: "The wife must respect her husband." For a wife to demand that her husband earn her respect would be like a man demanding the wife must earn his love. Both are wrong! Both men and women are to offer unconditionally the love and respect that the other so desperately wants and needs.

This is huge. Emerson Eggerichs, in his book *Love and Respect*, says, "Respect is a man's deepest value." He backed that statement up with research that he summarized this way:

> In one national study, four hundred men were given a choice between going through two negative experiences. If they were forced to choose one of the following, which would they prefer to endure?
>
> a) to be left alone and unloved in the world
> b) to feel inadequate and disrespected by everyone.
>
> Seventy-four percent of these men said that if they were forced to choose, they would prefer being alone and unloved in the world.[5]

The vast majority of men, nearly three quarters, chose to go without love because the foremost desire of the vast majority of men is for his woman to respect him. That respect is viewed by the godly man as a sign of her humble submission to God and him.

Returning to the case study, we find Boaz was startled in

the night, only to discover a woman at his feet.

**3:9 "Who are you?" he asked. "I am your servant Ruth,"
she said. "Spread the corner of your garment over me,
since you are a kinsman-redeemer."**

Notice that when asked, "Who are you?" Ruth calls
herself one of Boaz' "servants." She took both the posture
and title of a servant to show her profound respect for him.
After identifying herself, Ruth continued immediately by
saying the most curious thing: "Spread the corner of your
garment over me." What was this all about? Did she want to
sleep with him? If so, how could she be called a "virtuous
woman?" Of course she was not asking to sleep with him!
The phrase, "spread your covering" is descriptive of the
covenant of marriage. This same imagery will be used later by
Ezekiel to describe the LORD God's marriage to the nation
of Israel (Ezekiel 16:8). So Ruth was proposing to Boaz. Or
perhaps a bit more accurately, she was proposing that Boaz
propose to her. Quickly she added the justification for her
proposal that he propose to her: "since you are a kinsman-
redeemer."

This position of "kinsman-redeemer" was established by
God in the Law of Moses. You might say Ruth was getting
Biblical to keep everything on the up and up. Without getting
too sidetracked on the kinsman-redeemer, let's just say that a
kinsman-redeemer, in the time of the Judges, had two major
responsibilities: 1) to buy back relatives who had been sold
into slavery and to buy back their property as well;[6] and 2) to
marry the widow of your nearest kin if she was childless.[7] The
details of this will come to play later in this case study. For
now, the fact that Ruth has summoned the Biblical principle
of a kinsman-redeemer requires that Boaz act heroically, as a
"man of valor."

3:10 "The LORD bless you, my daughter," he replied.

Boaz responded with a prayer of blessing. Think about it. A younger woman, all dolled up, wearing a little of that "Moab Potion Number 9," comes to the single guy in the middle of the night saying, "Whatever you tell me I will do!"

He stopped to pray. Yes, to pray. The prayer here is in the form of a blessing. It is an invocation of God to visit Ruth with a blessing. In a normal prayer, the person praying takes someone else before God in prayer. But the blessing is a prayer that goes to God and asks God to visit the other person with a blessing. Let me suggest that praying is a great way to handle temptation. It is very difficult to act on a temptation when you are earnestly praying. Hebrews 2:18 tells us that Jesus "is able to help those who are being tempted." Again Hebrews 4:15-16 adds to this, "For we do not have a high priest who is unable to sympathize with our weaknesses, but we have one who has been tempted in every way, just as we are—yet was without sin. Let us then approach the throne of grace with confidence, so that we may receive mercy and find grace to help us in our time of need." Jesus will help if we will go to him for His help.

This is a great idea for dating people. Pray on your dates. Prayer time can be more intimate than a good-bye kiss. When two dating people pray, honestly from their hearts, they reveal who they truly are before God. They share their true heart's passion and desires. If you want to really know if the other is a person of valor or virtue, just listen to his or her prayers. They tell all.

If you want to really know if the other is a person of valor or virtue just listen to their prayers. They tell all.

Boaz then added…

3:10 … "This kindness is greater than that which you showed earlier: You have not run after the younger men, whether rich or poor."

Unfailing Love

Boaz referred to Ruth's "kindness." The word for "kindness," is frequently translated "unfailing love."[8] Several ideas are bound up in this word. The first idea is a love based in a covenant commitment.[9] The second is a love that is faithful to that covenant commitment.[10] The third is a love that endures forever.[11] These three aspects are what every godly single man desires in a woman. If a man is not interested in these qualities, it is a good sign that he is just not a godly single man. Boaz was. Boaz said that Ruth's present "unfailing love" was greater than that which Ruth showed earlier. So, when did Ruth show "unfailing love" earlier? Perhaps Boaz was referring to verse 2:11 where he said, "But I also know about the love and kindness you have shown your mother-in-law since the death of your husband...." (NLT). Now that statement actually rests on the covenant promise of verses 1:16-17. There Ruth promised under oath:

"Where you go I will go, and where you stay I will stay. Your people will be my people and your God my God. 17 Where you die I will die, and there I will be buried. May the LORD deal with me, be it ever so severely, if anything but death separates you and me."

Ruth's "unfailing love" was bound by a covenant. She had been faithful to it, and Boaz was aware that she meant it for life. But now this new "unfailing love" toward Boaz was greater than the earlier one. What was this new "unfailing love?" It was simply that she accepted Boaz, warts and all.

Every single godly man wants to be accepted for who he is.

Godly Men Want to be Accepted

Being accepted is another aspect of a virtuous woman that every single godly man wants. Every single godly man wants to be accepted for who he is.

In Boaz' case, it was to be accepted in spite of his age. There is no doubt that Boaz was significantly older than Ruth. He had repeatedly called Ruth, "My daughter." That Ruth would propose to him that he propose to her was unimaginable to him. He had precluded that he was too old to be considered by her. He must have pinched himself a couple of times to be sure he was not dreaming up this visit from Ruth. She accepted him for who he was—age and all.

Boaz continued his conversation with her that night by saying…

3:11 "… now, my daughter, don't be afraid. I will do for you all you ask. All my fellow townsmen know that you are a woman of noble character."

Boaz relieved any fear that Ruth may have had, that he might reject her. On top of that, he offered to do all she requested. That meant he would propose to her. Then Boaz gave the grounds for his action: she was a woman of equally good reputation to his own. What we have here are two "tens" who are planning to get married.

Godly Men Want Equality

Every single godly man is looking for equality in a woman. Not equality of the sexes—he's not looking for a macho woman. No, the equality he is looking for is spiritual equality. He is looking for a godly single woman. He knows he won't find her in the bar-hopping scene. In all likelihood, he will find her in church, worshipping and serving God.

Boaz had apparently waited for the right woman to come along, and perhaps due to his old age had even "given up" on the idea he would meet the right one. He wanted a woman of noble character, equal to his own, and wouldn't settle for less. Every single godly man wants a virtuous woman—a woman equally virtuous to his own valor (or more so); and that's what Boaz was getting in Ruth. You see, both

Boaz and Ruth were described by the same Hebrew word[12] translated "valor," when used of the male gender, and "virtue," when used of the female gender. In fact, they equally shared this quality. Neither one said, "Anyone will do. All I need is a spouse." The reason that neither would settle for less was because they themselves were people of valor/virtue. Sadly, not all today are willing to wait long enough for the person of valor/virtue to enter their life. Too many settle for less. Settling for less is a sure sign that you are not a person of valor/virtue. On the other hand, waiting on God to bring the right person into your life is a sure sign that you are a person of valor/virtue.

Waiting on God to bring the right person into your life is a sure sign that you are a person of valor/virtue.

Ruth's virtue was equal to Boaz', and everyone knew it. Ruth had developed a reputation of being virtuous. Nothing has changed today. Everyone has a reputation. Before seriously dating, you need to discover the reputation of the stranger who walked into your life. That reputation will be your first clue to whether or not he or she is a person of valor/virtue. What is the person's reputation according to those who really know him or her? Finding out the answer to that question will go a long way in sorting out who is the right person and who is not. In my years of dealing with singles, I have been approached by virtuous women who ask what I know about certain eligible single men. "Are they men of integrity?" On some occasions I have had to say, "Honestly, you can do better than that!" That was a polite way of saying, "NO!"

Godly Men Want to Solve Relationship Glitches

In the real world every relationship has its glitch. But this case study was too fairytale perfect. Everything was going too right. No one's life goes this smoothly. That's true. And it was true for Boaz and Ruth as well. Boaz added, "But there is one problem... (NLT)"

3:12 Although it is true that I am near of kin, there is a kinsman-redeemer nearer than I.

Obstacles in relationships are universal. Every relationship has it bumps, roadblocks, and detours that present difficulties to it. The obstacle set before Boaz and Ruth was huge because someone else could claim Naomi's property and take the bride ahead of Boaz. Naomi was aware of this, but she obviously did not inform Ruth. Naomi had hinted to it back in chapter 2:20. Regarding Boaz she said, "he is one of our kinsman-redeemers." Did you notice the plural? Boaz was just one of the kinsman-redeemers. What Naomi had dismissed or perhaps even deemed as insignificant, had now become a major problem to this relationship. Often it is the insignificant things that become huge obstacles later.

Every relationship has to have an "obstacle." The obstacle serves the purpose of affording an opportunity to demonstrate how each will handle a crisis or conflict. The obstacle shows up differently with every couple. For one couple the obstacle may be un-accepting parents or un-accepting children. For another it may a financial burden, health issues, or religious convictions. Obstacles appear in a relationship in order to test the couple with respect to their resolve to solve, enrich, and endure the problem, in order to advance the relationship.

> **Every relationship has to have an "obstacle."**

Boaz followed-up the bad news that there was a nearer kinsman-redeemer with compassionate good news. He said:

3:13 Stay here for the night, and in the morning if he wants to redeem, good; let him redeem. But if he is not

willing, as surely as the LORD lives I will do it. Lie here until morning."

He invited her to stay because it was not safe to go home in the dark. At daylight she would be much safer making the trip back to Naomi. The words that followed his invitation to stay may seem a little harsh, but really they are not. He said, "If he [the other kinsman-redeemer] wants to redeem you, good; let him redeem." How could Boaz have asserted that it would be "good?" Boaz could do so only because he accepted that it was God's sovereign hand that directed all the affairs of his life. This man of valor was willing to yield to God's sovereign plan. Boaz knew that if God's master plan called for placing Ruth into the arms of the other nearer kinsman-redeemer, then that would be fine with him. How could it be fine? Just remember that Boaz and Ruth have not crossed step 6 to step 7 of the 12 Steps in Bonding a Relationship for Life.

As will be seen later, Step 7 is the great divide. Intimate kissing begins at Step 7, and so does *deep* emotional involvement. Breaking up after crossing over to Step 7 is like a divorce or death all over again. But Boaz and Ruth had not gotten emotionally, physically, or sexually involved. As a result of that, even if the relationship should come to an end, neither one of them would have been severely crushed. Disappointed? Yes. Crushed? No. Why? It was because neither of them would have been ripped apart with chunks of each going with the other. That's because neither one crossed the line between Steps 6 and Step 7.

There is a lesson here for you, the reader. If you cross from Step 6 to Step 7 in a relationship, and the relationship goes sour, you will experience all the emotional pain that comes from the loss of a relationship. It will be just as if there was another separation by divorce or death. If, however, you don't cross the line between Steps 6 and 7 and the relationship doesn't work out, you will not experience the pain from the loss of relationship to such a severe degree.

Godly Men Want Trust

Couched in the language that Boaz used is the notion that he wanted Ruth to trust him on this one. This is yet another aspect of the virtuous woman that every single godly man wants. He wants a woman that will trust him and believe in him. Boaz appeared to be saying, "There's an obstacle, but trust me—I'll handle it." And trust him is what Ruth did.

3:14 So she lay at his feet until morning, but got up before anyone could be recognized; and he said, "Don't let it be known that a woman came to the threshing floor."

Boaz was such a man of valor that he would not have done anything that could be considered an impropriety or an immoral act. He would not have taken advantage of her. Boaz did remark that Ruth needed to keep their meeting a secret even though neither had done anything wrong. He didn't want anyone to know the relationship had become very serious. He was not trying to hide the relationship. He was just a very shrewd man with a strategy to handle the obstacle at hand. In all likelihood, he deemed that public knowledge of his interest in Ruth would only jeopardize his strategy. It would tip his hand and give the other (nearer) kinsman-redeemer the upper hand in negotiations for the "right of redemption."

Ruth had to trust his judgment on this and not question him.

In order to prove his integrity and show her that he would "do all that she had asked," he offered her a token ...

3:15 He also said, "Bring me the shawl you are wearing and hold it out." When she did so, he poured into it six measures of barley and put it on her. Then he went back to town.

Both Boaz and Ruth had left the threshing floor. Boaz went back to town, and Ruth went back to her mother-in-law. Of course, Ruth's return meant that she would be bombarded with a gazillion questions from Naomi about what happened. Her return went like this...

3:16 When Ruth came to her mother-in-law, Naomi asked, "How did it go, my daughter?" Then she told her everything Boaz had done for her 17 and added, "He gave me these six measures of barley, saying, 'Don't go back to your mother-in-law empty-handed.'"

Can you imagine all the chatter as Ruth told her everything in detail? Can you imagine Naomi's relief when she learned that her strategy had actually worked? Boaz proved himself to be truly a man of valor, who upheld his integrity when opportunity was afforded him to take advantage of Ruth.

Of all the things Ruth said to Naomi in that conversation, only one is recorded in this case study for us. It was recorded that Boaz gave her "six measures of barley, saying, 'Don't go back to your mother-in-law empty-handed.'" The Divine Case Worker included this so we would know that Boaz was wisely courting the "bitter" mother-in-law as well as Ruth. This is an important principle. You don't just date the person alone; you date the entire family. You can't get one without the other. You cannot separate your date from his or her family. It's a package deal!

Naomi understood that Boaz was courting her as well as Ruth because he was keenly interested in marrying Ruth. She could read people.

3:18 Then Naomi said, "Wait, my daughter, until you find out what happens. For the man will not rest until the matter is settled today."

Godly Men Want a Patient Woman

Naomi knew men well enough to know that now was the time to be relatively patient—that is, patient enough to give Boaz the time he needed to eliminate the obstacle. Naomi knew men are, by nature, problem-solvers. She knew in her heart that Boaz had a problem and that he would immediately set out to solve it. He just needed a little time. This is another aspect of the virtuous woman that every single godly man wants. He wants a woman who can be patient with him. He wants a woman who will give him the time to address the issue at hand and allow him to solve the matter in his way. That often requires patience on the woman's part, especially when she has her own plan in mind.

Be careful not to be confused here. Not all relationships are going somewhere. Naomi knew that Boaz would settle the matter as quickly as possible. She is not suggesting patience without limits on a man who will not make a commitment to the relationship nor do something about it. Too many singles are patiently waiting on someone who is all talk and no action or on someone who dates but will not commit. Naomi knew, from Ruth's report of everything that Boaz had said, that Boaz had promised to redeem Ruth if the nearer kinsman-redeemer would not do it. Knowing Boaz' integrity, Naomi was confident that he would certainly act as quickly as possible. Still, patience was required to give Boaz the time needed to eliminate the obstacle.

> **Too many singles are patiently waiting on someone who is all talk and no action or on someone who dates but will not commit.**

Godly Men Want to Contemplate Marriage

It is worth noticing that Boaz and Ruth were contemplating marriage and had only gone through Steps 1-6 of the 12 Steps in bonding a relationship for life. Of those six steps, Steps 4-6 had focused on world views and the compatibility of the two.

Steps 7-9 focus on facing each other. During the previous steps, the couple was postured side-by-side, and looked together outward, toward the world. They were sharing world views to see if they were compatible. Now in Steps 7-9 the couple looks toward each other. The focus is more on the non-verbal than on verbal communication. Intimate kissing takes place at this point and is the first step that introduces sexual arousal to the courting process. The relationship tends to move away from the intellectual process of verbal communication regarding world views and moves more toward an emotional and passionate process. Although sexual arousal takes place, there is no sexual contact during Steps 7-9.

Step 7 is called "Mouth to Mouth." It focuses on intimate kissing. Prior to this, only the casual greeting kind of kiss has taken place. But now intimate kissing takes place to prepare the couple for sex. Verbal communication and the intellectual side of the relationship slow down, as both emotions and passion pick up and take over.

A huge warning sign with a border of flashing lights needs to be posted at the Step 7 that says:

WARNING! When a couple moves from Step 6 to Step 7 they significantly increase the amount of pain they will experience upon a "break up" of the relationship.

Should a couple cross from Step 6 to Step 7, and then "break up," huge chunks of each person are ripped from them and go with the other person. This is similar to what happens in a separation, divorce, and death. People do not simply separate with a clean cut. No! Divorce and death are both a rough, painful, jagged tearing apart of two united lives. Pieces of each go with the other because they have emotionally and passionately given a part of themselves that cannot be taken back. The same is true for the dating couple who go beyond Step 6 to Step 7. Rarely do people who end the relationship after Step 7 maintain a friendship. The break-up will always be viewed as just too painful. However, those who break-up *before* Step 7 can go on to become best friends for life. So much is at stake here.

Boaz and Ruth did not cross to Step 7. So even if the other nearer kinsman-redeemer were to have stepped in and claimed his rights, neither Boaz nor Ruth would have been totally crushed. In fact, both would have been able to accept it with valor or virtue as the good hand of the true and living God's providential care for them.

Step 8 is called "Hand to Head." This step involves touching of the face, stroking the hair, tracing the edge of the ear, or cradling the head in one's lap. All are touches to the head which is considered our most vulnerable part of our body. To allow someone to touch the head indicates a profound trust of that person.

Step 9 is called "Hand to Body" because at this step there is a profound respect for the other's body. This is not done in a sexual way, but out of respect for the configuration of the other person's total make up. This includes imperfections and idiosyncrasies that are accepted, even appreciated, because they make that person who they are.

Obviously Boaz and Ruth saved all the steps from 7-12 for marriage. What they did is not our cultural norm. It is our twenty-first century practice, at least among Christians, to go through all the steps, up to 9, and reserve Steps 10-12 for marriage. The non-Christians in our culture rarely reserve anything for marriage. They often move in and co-habit even though such actions increase the likelihood of divorce by around 50% more when they do marry.[13] Hollywood, TV, and the entertainment industry promote Steps 1-3, skipping Steps 4-9, and picking up with Steps 10-12 in nearly every romance movie, sit-com, and reality show (See Chart 2). Their version goes like this: scene one, guy meets girl; scene two, guy and girl are in bed together. It's no wonder that those relationships don't last—they have not bonded for life. Donald Joy writes:

> In Desmond Morris' book, *Intimate Behavior*, he reports that the Twelve Steps in pair bonding tend to be present in all human cultures. He notes that variation from the Twelve Steps tend to move people toward more violent sexual behavior. Morris cautions that when steps are missed in the rush to genital intimacy, the bond tends to be deformed and to break.[14]

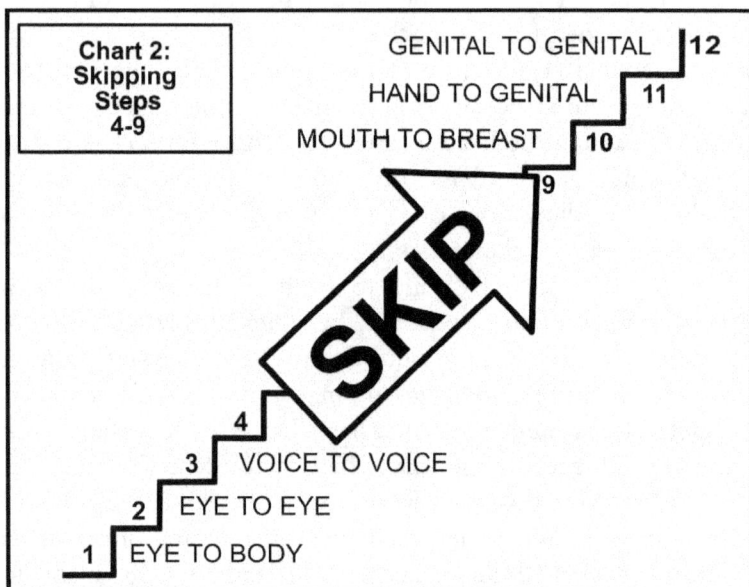

Chart 2:
Skipping
Steps
4-9

GENITAL TO GENITAL | 12
HAND TO GENITAL | 11
MOUTH TO BREAST | 10
9

SKIP

4
3 | VOICE TO VOICE
2 | EYE TO EYE
1 | EYE TO BODY

The last three steps are all intended for marriage because they are sexual in nature. They need little clarification and are as follows:

Step 10 is called "Mouth to Breast." The intimate kissing that started at Step 7 was the beginning of sexual arousal.

Such arousal when piqued will ultimately lead to foreplay and caressing of the breasts that characterize Step 10.

Step 11 is called "Hand to Genital." With sexual arousal under way the hands spontaneously seek out to caress the final source of pleasure.

Step 12 is called "Genital to Genital." With both fully aroused, sexual penetration in the act of marriage takes place.

It is clear from the case study that both Boaz and Ruth were saving all of the Steps 7-12 for marriage. What are you saving?

Chapter Three Notes

[1] The Hebrew expression for "woman of virtue" is אשת חיל *(asheth khayil)*.

[2] This provides further evidence that the term "valor" had nothing to do with wealth or nobility, as some translations render it. Such a rendering appears to be based on 2 Kings 15:20 which correctly rendered it as "mighty men of wealth." By the time of 2 Kings, the concept had broadened metaphorically to the idea of mighty warrior in the market (so-to-speak). However, reading a much later usage into this early usage does not fit because the author of Ruth used the exact same term for Ruth who was a cash poor foreigner. Since the same term is used for both Boaz and Ruth by the same author, in the same book, it is clear that the author intended the term be understood the same way for both. What this means is that translating the word as "man of standing" (NIV) or "mighty man of wealth" (KJV) for Boaz in chapter 2:1 just does not fit. Why? Because that translation just does not work on the flip side for Ruth. She was clearly not wealthy! She was a beggar. Obviously, the rendering of this term in a financial or social class way is misleading. Both Boaz and Ruth possessed the quality of "valor/virtue." Again, we suggest that the focus was on the internal quality that overcame the obstacles and hardships of life through faith in the living God. Both Boaz and Ruth had that internal quality as the TWOT suggests: "When the term is used of a woman (Ruth 3:11; Prov 12:4; and 31:10) it is translated "virtuous" (ASV, RSV, "worthy" or "good"), but it may be that a woman of this caliber had all the attributes of her male counterpart." TWOT, vol. 1, pp. 271-2.

[3] Dennis Henderson, *Living Single Again*, (a seven-part DVD videos series), Single Initiative, 2005.

The *Living Single Again* DVD series is a post-divorce recovery program. While divorce recovery programs focus on healing past emotional and relational wounds, *Living Single Again* focuses on developing future relationships in a Biblical way that will not repeat past failures. *Living Single Again* is available online at: http://www.LivingSingleAgain.com.

⁴ The 25 times the expression "at his feet" occurs in the NIV are: Ruth 3:7, 8, 14; 1 Samuel 25:24; 2 Samuel 4:12; 2 Kings 4:27,37; Esther 8:3; Job 9:13; Matthew 15:30; Mark 5:22; 7:25; Luke 7:38; 8:28, 35,41, 47; John 11:32; Acts 5:2,10; 10:25; Hebrews 2:8; Revelation 1:17; 19:10. In spite of the fact that there is no support from within the Scriptures for attributing that something sexual took place when lying at the feet, there are those who try to read into this passage some act of immorality. That just does not fit with the attribute of valor/virtue that the author made so preeminent in the narrative. At best, the sexual concept has to be imported from pagan cultures and attributed to these virtuous people. That is not a very convincing argument.

⁵ Emmerson Eggerichs, *Love & Respect*, Integrity, 2004. p. 49.

⁶ The concept of the kinsman-redeemer embraced more than repurchasing a family member and his or her property, it included avenging as well (Numbers 35:12-34; Deuteronomy 19:1-3). The concept that played out in the case study of Boaz and Ruth focused primarily on the aspect of the Mosaic Law concerning property. The laws governing the redemption of property are found chiefly in Leviticus 25:23-55 and also within the laws regarding the Year of Jubilee. This is addressed in the fourth chapter of Ruth.

⁷ Levirate Marriage (called *Yibum* in Hebrew) was an institution that required a man to marry the childless widow of his brother to produce a child who would carry on the deceased brother's name, so that the deceased brother's name would not be forgotten. Deuteronomy 25:5-10 gives the details of this kind of marriage. This will be addressed in the fourth chapter of Ruth.

A question often raised is "would not the levirate marriage law of Deuteronomy 25:5-10 lead to incest or polygamy, if the nearest kinsman-redeemer were already married?" Of course God would not offer a law that would contradict His other laws. This law must be understood in harmony with the other stipulations of the law. Therefore, it was the nearest "single" brother or relative that would be qualified to act as the levirate husband.

8 The word חסד *hesed* is translated in the NIV as "unfailing love" thirty times for God's love (Exodus 15:13; Ps. 6:4; 13:5; 21:7; 31:16; 32:10; 33:5, 18, 22; 36:7; 44:26; 48:9; 51:1; 52:8; 77:8; 85:7; 90:14; 107:8, 15, 21, 31; 119:41, 76; 130:7; 143:8, 12; 147:11; 54:10; Lam 3:32; Hos 10:12) and twice for man's love (Pro 19:22; 20:6).

9 The idea of covenant is illustrated by Jeremiah 2:2 where the חסד *hesed* of Israel's youth is likened to the love of a bride (in a marriage covenant). Other's have seen the whole idea of *hesed* love as grounded in covenant (see Nelson Glueck , *Hesed in the Bible*, 1927). Perhaps that is why in Ruth 3:10 it is rendered "loyalty" in the NLT.

10 A form of the word חסד *hesed* is used with a form of the word אמת *emeth* some twenty-five times in the Old Testament, to reinforce the veracity of the commitment of love. As such, it means "faithful love."

11 See note 8 above.

12 The same Hebrew word חיל (*khayil*--valor/virtue) was used by the author to describe both Ruth and Boaz. (See the Note 2 above).

13 Nadya Labi, "A Bad Start," *Time*, February 15, 1999. Nadya reported on the National Marriage Project, a group committed to "revitalizing marriage," based at Rutgers University in New Jersey. In this article Naday wrote, "Cohabiting couples are more likely to experience a host of domestic problems-- including, if they finally get married, divorce. Cohabiting unions tend to weaken the institution of marriage and pose clear and present dangers for women and children." The article continued, "The report contends that cohabitation reduces the likelihood of later wedded bliss. It quotes a 1992 study of 3,300 adults showing that those who had lived with a partner were 46% more likely to divorce than those who had not. 'The longer you cohabit, the

more tolerant you are of divorce,' says David Popenoe, the sociologist who co-wrote the study."

Researcher after researcher has concluded that the risk of divorce after having cohabited before marriage is significantly higher than the risk of divorce after marrying and not having co-habited previously. For example, "The overall association between premarital cohabitation and subsequent marital stability is striking. The dissolution rate of women who cohabit prematurely with their future spouse is, on the average, nearly 80 percent higher than the rate of those who do not" (Neil Bennett, Ann Blanc and David Bloom, "Commitment and Modern Union: Assessing the Link Between Premarital Cohabitation and Subsequent Marital Stability," *American Sociology Review* 53 (1988): 127-138).

[14] Joy, *Bonding*, p.41.

Part Four:
"Lord, What Do You Want for Single People?"

It's Not Hard to Figure Out

God wants to redeem you and to bless you. Sometimes that's hard to believe. Nevertheless, it's true. He did that for both Ruth and Boaz and He wants to do that for you. These ideas of redemption and blessing are so important that the Divine Case Worker devoted the entire fourth chapter to them. God's desire to redeem is clearly seen from the 13 times a form of the word "redeem" occurs in this chapter alone (and the 21 times a form of "redeem" occurs in the entire case study). The word "redeem" is a financial term that means to "purchase" or "buy" something.[1] We will see that God wants to buy us out of our spiritual destitution, enslavement to sin, and hardship of life.

God Wants to Redeem Your Life

The concept of a "kinsman-redeemer" was developed in the Old Testament with two aspects. The first aspect was to buy back property that a relative had sold when he or she found him or herself destitute (selling oneself into slavery as property of another was also included as property that could be bought back). The second aspect was to marry the widow of a family member who died without an heir in order to father a child who would carry on the dead relative's family line. Though both these ideas were not originally found together—by the time of the Judges, the two concepts had merged.

Beneath all this stood a foundational principle that God owned all property. Therefore, the so-called "owners" were only "tenants" on God's property. Leviticus 25 puts it this way:

> [23] "The land must not be sold permanently, because the land is mine and you are but aliens and my tenants. [24] Throughout the country that you hold as a possession, you must provide for the redemption of the land."

Consequently, the possession of the land was to be regulated by God's laws, since he was the ultimate Owner. Leviticus 25 goes on to say:

> [25] "If one of your countrymen becomes poor and sells some of his property, **his nearest relative is to come and redeem what his countryman has sold. ...** [28] But if he does not acquire the means to repay him, what he sold will remain in the possession of the buyer **until the Year of Jubilee**. It will be returned in the Jubilee, and he can then go back to his property." [Bold added]

According to the bolded passages above, it is clear that the nearest kin was given the first right to redeem property. From the Case Study it appears that Naomi and Elimelech had owned property that apparently had been sold when they left for Moab a little over ten years earlier. That land would go back to Naomi in the Year of Jubilee (which occurred every fifty years).[2]

According to the Mosaic Law, the *price* of redeeming the

land would be contingent on the length of time left until the Year of Jubilee: more for a longer contract of ownership and less for a shorter contract of ownership.³ Furthermore, the people who qualified as kinsman-redeemer appear to have had a rank or order in which they could step in and redeem. The first right went to the original owner and then to a brother and then to: "An uncle or a cousin or any blood relative in his clan" (Leviticus 25:49). So the first principle underlying the concept of a kinsman-redeemer is that God owns the land and had detailed rules for the tenants who possessed His land.

The second principle regarding a kinsman-redeemer was simply that the land needed an heir to whom the land would go back in the Year of Jubilee. The question was, "If the owner died without a child, how would the land go back to the original owner's family?" Well, to solve this dilemma another law found in Deuteronomy 25 was applied to the property law. Deuteronomy 25:5-10 says,

> ⁵ If brothers are living together and one of them dies without a son, his widow must not marry outside the family. Her husband's brother shall take her and marry her and fulfill the duty of a brother-in-law to her. ⁶ The first son she bears shall carry on the name of the dead brother so that his name will not be blotted out from Israel. ⁷ However, if a man does not want to marry his brother's wife, she shall go to the elders at the town gate and say, "My husband's brother refuses to carry on his brother's name in Israel. He will not fulfill the duty of a brother-in-law to me." ⁸ Then the elders of his town shall summon him and talk to him. If he persists in saying, "I do not want to marry her," ⁹ his brother's widow shall go up to him in the presence of the elders, take off one of his sandals, spit in his face and say, "This is what is done to the man who will not build up his brother's family line." ¹⁰ That man's line shall be known in

Israel as The Family of the Unsandaled.

According to the merging of these two passages, the kinsman-redeemer was not only to buy the land but also, if there was no heir, to take the landowner's widow as a wife in order to have a child who would be reckoned as the child of the dead man, and that child would become heir of the land.

One more feature surfaces from the above Deuteronomy passage and is significant as background material for our case study. There were different kinds of kinsman-redeemers. They are identified as:

1] The Unsandaled Kinsman-Redeemer – He was able to redeem because he had sufficient resources to buy the land but was *not* willing to redeem the woman.

2] The Extra-Sandaled Kinsman-Redeemer – He was able to redeem the land and he was also willing to redeem the woman.

3] and of course the Unable Kinsman-Redeemer – He was not able to redeem (he was cash poor) and so it didn't matter if he was willing or not. He did not have the financial wherewithal to redeem.

All this provides crucial background material as we pick up with the fourth chapter of this case study. Remember that as we left the Chapter three of Ruth, Boaz was on his way to town.

God Wants Singles to Have a Strategy

4:1 Meanwhile Boaz went up to the town gate and sat there. When the kinsman-redeemer he had mentioned came along, Boaz said, "Come over here, my friend, and sit down." So he went over and sat down.

Boaz headed to the town gate because that was the place where official legal business transactions took place. He had come up with a strategy to redeem the property of Elimelech, even though he was not the nearest kinsman-redeemer. He was on a mission with a clearly defined goal and strategy. When it came to strategy, Boaz was like a master chess player who has all his moves planned out before he made the first one. Boaz was convinced that in as few as five moves he could have the nearest kinsman-redeemer in check-mate. His plan to do so revolved around a real estate transaction. So once he and the nearer kinsman-redeemer were at the town gate, where real estate transactions took place, he was ready to implement the first move of his strategy.

He was on a mission with a clearly defined goal and strategy.

Boaz' **FIRST MOVE** was to summon the Elders as witnesses:

4:2 Boaz took ten of the elders of the town and said, "Sit here," and they did so.

Meeting with the Elders followed the legal format of the day. [4] Boaz had to have witnesses of the levirate marriage transaction. He may have only needed three. But if three was good—then ten was better. Obviously, Boaz wanted the forthcoming transaction to be indisputable.

Boaz' **SECOND MOVE** was to propose a real estate deal that the nearer kinsman-redeemer could not refuse.

3 Then he said to the kinsman-redeemer, "Naomi, who has come back from Moab, is selling the piece of land that belonged to our brother Elimelech. 4 I thought I should bring the matter to your attention and suggest that you buy it in the presence of these seated here and in the presence of the elders of my people. If you will

redeem it, do so. But if you will not, tell me, so I will know. For no one has the right to do it except you, and I am next in line." "I will redeem it," he said.

In Boaz' conversation with the nearer kinsman-redeemer, he has called Elimelech "our brother." That may have meant "brother," in a broader sense of the word, as merely any "relative." But in all likelihood, he was actually their "brother." Boaz and the unnamed nearer kinsman-redeemer were Naomi's brothers-in-law; and it appears that Boaz was the younger of the three (or more) brothers because he was not the nearest kinsman-redeemer.

The text appears to be saying that Naomi was selling the land. However, the study note on this passage in the NET Bible suggests that:

> The nature of the sale is uncertain. Naomi may have been selling the property rights to the land, but this seems unlikely in light of what is known about ancient Israelite property laws. It is more likely that Naomi, being a woman, held only the right to use the land until the time of her remarriage or death (F. W. Bush, *Ruth, Esther* [WBC], 202-4). Because she held this right to use of the land, she also had the right to buy it back from its current owner. (This assumes that Elimelech sold the land prior to going to Moab.) Since she did not possess the means to do so, however, she decided to dispose of her rights in the matter. She was not selling the land per se, but disposing of the right to its redemption and use, probably in exchange for room and board with the purchaser (Bush, 211-15). If this is correct, it might be preferable to translate, "Naomi is disposing of her rights to the portion of land," although such a translation presumes some knowledge of ancient Israelite property laws.[5]

You see, if Naomi had had the money, she would have had first right to buy back the land. Since she did not have the money, she was "selling" her right to the land to her kinsman-redeemer.

Boaz, in a very business-like manner, concealed his real intention to marry Ruth. Boaz suggested that the nearer kinsman-redeemer buy the land. Boaz also informed him that if he chose not to buy it, then Boaz himself would buy it in the presence of all the witnesses. His strategy was to entice the nearer kinsman-redeemer to think that if Boaz, the mighty man of valor, desired the land, then it must be a good deal.

Without hesitation, the nearer kinsman-redeemer jumped on the opportunity to buy the land. "I will redeem it," he said. Now Boaz had him where he wanted him.

Boaz' **THIRD MOVE** counted on the nearer kinsman-redeemer jumping on the opportunity to buy the land. His third move was to hit the nearer kinsman-redeemer with the lien against the property:

5 Then Boaz said, "On the day you buy the land from Naomi and from Ruth the Moabitess, you acquire the dead man's widow, in order to maintain the name of the dead with his property."

What a surprise for the nearer kinsman-redeemer. He just agreed to buy the property and now Boaz laid on him the fact that there was a lien against the property. The lien was rather significant, too. It required taking care of the bitter widow, Naomi, and marrying the widow, Ruth, who had no heir. Boaz knew that this was his trump card. Why? Because with the marriage also came the responsibility to father a child through the widow in order to raise an heir to the property. Just as Boaz expected, the nearer kinsman-redeemer had second thoughts:

6 At this, the kinsman-redeemer said, "Then I cannot redeem it because I might endanger my own estate.

You redeem it yourself. I cannot do it."

The nearer kinsman-redeemer realized that this deal would put his own first-born heir's inheritance in jeopardy. How so is not clear. Perhaps this meant that the inheritance of his other children (if he had any) or future children would be diminished.[6]

When the nearer kinsman-redeemer said, "I cannot redeem it," he was not totally accurate. To say, "I cannot," implied he was incapacitated to redeem it; that he did not have the ability to do so because he did not have the money. In reality, he did have the capacity and ability to do so—he just didn't want to. It was not that he could not—it was that he would not. He was not willing to fulfill his God-ordained role and accept the will of God to redeem the land and the widow. He didn't want to because that would have led in the direction of potentially bumping his own heir from the prominent position of first-born heir. It appears that the child that potentially could come from a union with the sister-in-law would have first claim. He was no different than any of us when the will of God goes counter to our own plans. Single-again people often have an extremely difficult time accepting God's plan for singleness and prefer to get back into a relationship. Instead of viewing singleness as a gift from God and a time to focus on healing, they look for a new relationship. They rationalize that if I only had a relationship I would be much happier. As a result, they impede the recovery process. They hinder the healing process of getting over the previous relationship. With regard to waiting on God for someone, over and over I have heard singles say, "I can't." "I need someone." What they really are saying is, "I won't." So off into the dating arena they go. There

> **Sometimes we must choose the more difficult path to receive God's greater blessing on the other end.**

is a huge difference between "I cannot" and "I won't." This nearer kinsman-redeemer could have redeemed. He had the ability, but he would not, because it was a hardship for him. Sometimes we must choose the more difficult path to receive God's greater blessing on the other end. He did not, and Boaz had anticipated that he would not. You might say the nearer kinsman-redeemer was rather predictable. How about you?

Boaz' strategy led right into his **FOURTH MOVE.** The fourth move was to allow the nearer kinsman-redeemer to back out of the deal, just as the law had allowed with a disgraceful penalty. It is always a disgrace to shirk one's responsibility.

7 (Now in earlier times in Israel, for the redemption and transfer of property to become final, one party took off his sandal and gave it to the other. This was the method of legalizing transactions in Israel.)

Notice that the above parenthesis is another Divine Case Worker insertion. The Divine Case Worker summed up all the rules set forth in both Leviticus and Deuteronomy regarding the redemption and transfer of property in two sentences. The first sentence revealed that a token was involved—kind of like a seal on a document. The one giving up the property handed over his sandal to seal the deal. Accepting the sandal meant that the property and liens against it were officially the obligation of the sandal holder. That was the method of legalizing the sale of property. This parenthetic material, inserted by the Divine Case Worker, only summarizes the deal. The details of the real estate deal, in all likelihood, included more than is recorded. For example, according to Mosaic Law, when a kinsman-redeemer was unwilling to redeem the property, the widow was required to spit in his face and remove his sandal. He was to be un-sandaled as a public disgrace (Deuteronomy 25:7-10). From what is mentioned by the Divine Case

Worker, we can be sure that nearer kinsman-redeemer was disgraced by reneging on the deal and his responsibility. Such "disgrace" is evident by the fact that the nearer kinsman-redeemer is never mentioned by name—not even once. That was to fulfill the words of Deuteronomy 25:10 that he shall be known, not by his name, but as the "Unsandaled" and that his heirs be known as the "family of the Unsandaled." It is always a disgraceful thing to know God's will and not do it.

8 So the kinsman-redeemer said to Boaz, "Buy it yourself." And he removed his sandal.

The *FIFTH MOVE* in the strategy of Boaz was to buy the land himself and accept the lien against the land with joy! That's exactly what Boaz did:

9 Then Boaz announced to the elders and all the people, "Today you are witnesses that I have bought from Naomi all the property of Elimelech, Kilion and Mahlon. 10 I have also acquired Ruth the Moabitess, Mahlon's widow, as my wife, in order to maintain the name of the dead with his property, so that his name will not disappear from among his family or from the town records. Today you are witnesses!"

God Wants Singles to Relate Everything to Jesus

Historically, Christian writers and preachers have seen Boaz as a type or precursor to the ultimate kinsman-redeemer: Jesus.

Boaz exemplified what a true kinsman-redeemer should be. Historically, both Christian authors and preachers have seen Boaz as a type or precursor to the ultimate kinsman-redeemer: Jesus. Boaz prefigured Christ in at least seven ways:

1. Boaz Was a Near Kin Just As Christ is Our Near Kin.

Just as Boaz had to be kin to Elimelech and Mahlon to redeem the land and the widow, so the ultimate Redeemer had to be of mankind. Hebrews 2:17 states clearly regarding the ultimate messianic kinsman-redeemer, "For this reason he had to be made like his brothers in every way, in order that he might become a merciful and faithful high priest in service to God, and that he might make atonement for the sins of the people." A priest has to be human. An angel would not do. Therefore, an angel cannot redeem. An angel cannot pay the price of mankind's redemption. Neither could an animal sacrifice take the place of the sinner and "take away" his or her sins. Hebrews 10:4 explains "because it is impossible for the blood of bulls and goats to take away sins." The redeemer had to be of mankind. That's exactly what Jesus is. He is God, the second person of the eternal trinity, who became flesh (John 1:1-3, 14). God joined with His divine nature, a human nature in order to qualify as the Redeemer Who would save us from our sins and bring us to Himself.

2. Boaz Was Able to Pay the Debt Just As Christ Was Able to Pay Our Debt.

It was not enough to be kin. Boaz also had to have the wherewithal to pay the redemption price. Had Boaz been destitute or a slave himself, he would not have been able to pay the price and redeem the land and the widow. But in fact he was able. Likewise, our redeemer had to be more than just another fallen sinful part of mankind. For all mankind has been enslaved to sin by one sinful act that we call the fall of Adam (Romans 3:23; 5:12). Adam's corruption has been passed down to every descendent. So none of mankind is righteous nor in good standing to serve as a redeemer (Romans 3:10-12). The consequence of that one act of rebellion against God was lethal. All humankind became obligated to pay the price that justice required. The price was, and still is, death: "For the wages of sin is death" (Romans 6:23). Since all mankind is sinful, and consequently unable to pay their own debt, no one can pay anyone else's debt—because everyone is obligated to pay their own.

The only hope of redemption is found in Jesus. The Holy Spirit overshadowed the Virgin Mary so that she conceived a child. The Holy Spirit's overshadowing and the Power of the Most High protected Jesus from the pollutions of sin, so that the child born was "holy" in the fullest sense of being without sin (Luke 1:35). Born sinless, He then lived a sinless life that qualified Him to be the Redeemer. Of Jesus, God says, He "had no sin," "committed no sin," "and in Him is no sin" (2 Corinthians 5:21; 1 Peter 2:22; 1 John 3:5). He was called the sacrificial "lamb without blemish or defect." He alone is qualified to be the Redeemer of the world. The New Testament says, "Therefore he is able to save completely those who come to God through him" (Hebrews 7:25).

3. Boaz Was Willing to Pay the Debt Just As Christ Was Willing to Pay Our Debt.

It was not enough to qualify as kin to the person in need of redemption and be able to redeem. The redeemer had to be willing to redeem—willing to pay the price. Boaz could have chosen to be as unwilling as the Unsandaled redeemer, but instead he was willing to redeem—he chose to redeem. Likewise, Jesus qualified as our kinsman-redeemer, but it was necessary that he be willing to redeem. He could have said, "Father, I don't want to redeem the sorry lot of sinful humanity," in which case we would all have been left to our miserable condition of doom. But instead, Jesus said regarding his own life, "No one takes it from me, but I lay it down of my own accord. I have authority to lay it down and authority to take it up again" (John 10:18). Jesus voluntarily stepped in as our kinsman-redeemer and he did so motivated by love (Ephesians 5:22), just as Boaz voluntarily redeemed

Ruth, motivated by love.

4. Boaz Paid the Redemption Price Just As Christ Paid in Full Our Redemption Price.

Just suppose the kin was both qualified and willing to redeem but was just a little short on cash. Well, the redemption would not take place. The price had to be paid in full. That is exactly what Jesus Christ did for those for whom he died. He paid in full the price of sin. On the cross Jesus uttered, ""It is finished."[7] That was a common expression in the time of Christ that meant that the debt had been "paid in full." Jesus paid in full the price with His sacrifice of Himself as our substitute. The wage of sin was death, and He took our place. He both offered the sacrifice as a priest and was the sacrifice. He voluntarily offered Himself. He died in the place of the guilty (1 Corinthians 5:21; 1 Peter 2:34; 3:18), so the guilty could go away freely pardoned. 1 Peter 1 says:

> 18 For you know that it was not with perishable things such as silver or gold that **you were redeemed** from the empty way of life handed down to you from your forefathers, 19 but **with the precious blood of Christ**, a lamb without blemish or defect. (Bold added)

5. Boaz Graced Ruth Just As Christ Graced the Church.

Boaz did it all. Ruth could only accept the gracious redemption that her kinsman-redeemer provided. Likewise, Christ did it all. We can only accept the merit of what He did. We can add nothing to it—nor take anything from it. The apostle Paul said it this way: "For it is by grace you have been saved, through faith— and this not from yourselves, it is the gift of God—not by works, so that no one can boast (Ephesians 2:8-9). The term "grace" means it was unearned, unmerited, and undeserved. Grace means God's salvation is a gift that is freely bestowed. Salvation from our sinful condition is totally a work of our Redeemer, Jesus Christ. Accepting Him is the only way to be saved (John 14:6; Acts 4:12; 1 Timothy 2:5).

Trying to earn salvation or trying to reform your life is totally void of any value by the fact that it is "—not by works, so that no one can boast." You must accept Christ's redemption alone, just as Ruth accepted Boaz' redemption alone. You accept Christ's work of redemption by calling on Him to save you (Romans 10:13). You call out in a prayer that comes from your heart—in which you admit your guiltiness of sin (1 John 1:9). You also must believe from your heart that Jesus Christ died and rose again from the dead to redeem you from your sins (Romans 10:9, 10). It's not hard to do. I called on Jesus as an eight year old boy with the simplest of prayer, and He saved me. Just call on Him now in prayer, and He will save you, too.

6. Boaz Took Ruth to be His Bride Just As Christ Took the Church to be His Bride.

Boaz publicly proposed to Ruth and announced his engagement to her at the same time: "Today you are witnesses that I have ... acquired Ruth the Moabitess, Mahlon's widow, as my wife...." Boaz took Ruth as his bride—his wife. Likewise, the relationship of Christ to the church is one of a groom to a bride and a husband to a wife. In Ephesians 5, dealing with the husband and wife relationship, it says:

> 25 Husbands, love your wives, just as Christ loved the church and gave himself up for her 26 to make her holy, cleansing her by the washing with water through the word, 27 and to present her to himself as a radiant church, without stain or wrinkle or any other blemish, but holy and blameless.

7. Boaz Redeemed the Land Just As Christ Ultimately Will Redeem the Earth.

Boaz both redeemed the land and took Ruth to be his wife. Likewise, Christ redeems His people, and ultimately the curse on the earth will be lifted as well. In Romans 8, Paul indicates that the earth itself was subjected to frustration by the fall of man into sin and that ultimately in the age to come, when the believer's body is redeemed, the earth will be liberated too. Paul says in Romans 8:

> 20 For the creation was subjected to frustration, not by its own choice, but by the will of the one who subjected it, in hope 21 that the creation itself will be liberated from its bondage to decay and brought into the glorious freedom of the children of God. 22 We know that the whole creation has been groaning as in the pains of childbirth right up to the present time. 23 Not only so, but we ourselves, who have the firstfruits of the Spirit, groan inwardly as we wait eagerly for our adoption as sons, the redemption of our bodies.

The Church Prefigured by Ruth

Not only does Boaz prefigure Christ but Ruth prefigures the Church as well. There are at least seven ways in which Ruth does so:

1. Ruth Was a Moabitess Who Did *NOT* Belong to Boaz' People Just As Many of the People in the Church were Gentiles Who Did *NOT* Belong to God's People.

Ruth was a Moabitess. She was a foreigner—an alien. She had been an idolater. She was not of God's people. In a similar way, Paul speaking of the church says in Ephesians 2:

11 Therefore, remember that formerly you who are Gentiles by birth and called "uncircumcised" by those who call themselves "the circumcision" (that done in the body by the hands of men)—12 remember that at that time you were separate from Christ, excluded from citizenship in Israel and foreigners to the covenants of the promise, without hope and without God in the world. 13 But now in Christ Jesus you who once were far away have been brought near through the blood of Christ.... 19 Consequently, you are no longer foreigners and aliens, but fellow citizens with God's people and members of God's household....

We who are gentiles were not God's people, but through the redemption that is in Christ, we became the people of God. The point here is that no matter what your circumstances, if you do not turn back like Orpah did, and turn to the Lord as Ruth did, when you come to the Lord He accepts you and makes you one of his very own. Turn to Him now!

2. Ruth Was Destitute and So Was the Church Before Christ Bought Her.

Ruth came with nothing. She was poor and destitute. She had nothing to offer Boaz. Likewise, every person who comes to Christ must acknowledge his or her spiritual destitution. Romans 3:10-12 tells us about our true spiritual condition:

10 "There is no one righteous, not even one; 11 there is no one who understands, no one who seeks God. 12 All have turned away, they have together become worthless; there is no one who does good, not even one."

In Ephesians 2:1 the spiritual condition of people before becoming Christians is even gloomier: "As for you, you were dead in your transgressions and sins." This verse indicates that we were so destitute spiritually, that we were pronounced "dead." Obviously, dead people are not able to do anything—that's the very point. Spiritually we were void of anything that could merit us to God. Just as Ruth needed Boaz to redeem her, we need the ultimate Redeemer, Jesus Christ, to redeem us.

3. Ruth Believed in Boaz and So Does the True Church Believe in Jesus Christ.

Ruth believed in Boaz (and so did Naomi). Their belief in him was more than just a mental assent that he could or even would redeem. Their faith went beyond the brain and moved to the heart, in actions that showed they believed in Boaz. Likewise, a person today must believe with the heart to be saved. Romans 10:9, 10 says:

> 9 That if you confess with your mouth, "Jesus is Lord," and **believe in your heart that God raised him from the dead, you will be saved.** 10 **For it is with your heart that you believe and are justified,** and it is with your mouth that you confess and are saved. (Bold added)

Just verbally saying, "I believe," won't do—if it only comes from the head as an acknowledgement of facts alone. Someone might say, "Sure, I believe Jesus is the Son of God." Or say, "I believe that Jesus died on the cross." And as grand as that is, if it is only an acknowledgment of the historical fact and comes only from the head, it may fall twelve inches too short—the distance between the brain and the heart. You must "believe in your heart" with a faith that takes a course of action and confesses that Jesus is your Lord.

If Ruth and Naomi had only believed in their heads, they would have said, "I know he is able to redeem and he is willing to redeem" and done nothing about it. But because they believed in their hearts, they acted on what they knew.

Naomi planned and Ruth acted on the plan because they believed in their hearts that Boaz was both able and willing to redeem. So it is with salvation faith. You must know it in your head and believe in your heart. You must call on the name of the Lord to save you from your sins and trust Him to do so!

4. Ruth Received a Whole New Life and So Does the Church.

From Moab to the "House of Bread," from poverty to wealth, and from being a widow to being a wife, Ruth had a whole new life. The same is true for the believer in Christ—everything changes when you become a believer "in Christ." The apostle Paul put it this way in 2 Corinthians 5:17, "Therefore, if anyone is in Christ, he is a new creation; the old has gone, the new has come!"

When Christians tell someone about the change that took place at the time of accepting Christ as Savior, they are giving their "testimony." This testimony usually includes a three-part conversation. The first part shares how meaning-lessness life was before Christ. The second part gives the details of how someone introduced them to Christ. The final part discusses all the radical changes that occurred after calling on Christ for salvation. Most who give this kind of testimony would agree that the change was not intentional on their part. By that they mean that they did not set out to change. They hadn't planned on any change. Change somehow occurred because Christ altered everything in life. He changed the person from the inside out. Now, imagine the testimony Ruth could share about her former life in Moab before Boaz (the old life), how she met and married Boaz, and her life now after the marriage to Boaz (the new life). Everything changed because of him—just as everything changes because of Christ.

5. Ruth Became a Part of a Whole New Family Just As in the Church Believers Become a Part of a Whole New Family.

Ruth was no longer in Moab. She was now no longer Ms. Ruth. She was now Mrs. Boaz of Bethlehem. Soon she would have a son. This was a whole new family. Likewise, when a person accepts Christ as Savior, he or she is born into a whole new family. 1 Peter 4:16 refers to this family as "the family of God."

6. Ruth Was Blessed Just As the Church is Blessed.

God blessed Ruth, and she immediately conceived. After ten years of trying to have a child with her first husband Mahlon, she had none. But then on the first night of her honeymoon she conceived (see Ruth 4:13). What a huge blessing. Likewise, non-Christians seek blessings in life, but something is always missing. It's because they have a God-sized hole in their hearts—which only God can fill. Single-again people try to fill that hole with whatever they can—relationships, careers, family, entertainment, possessions, success, and on and on. But they are still empty. This vacuum in life can only be filled by "Christ, who has blessed us in the heavenly realms with every spiritual blessing in Christ" (Ephesians 1:3). Christ is all you need to be truly blessed.

7. Ruth Found Herself in a New Home Just As the Church Will Find Herself in a New Home.

There's no question that marrying Boaz meant a step up in living conditions and a new home for Ruth. The same is true for the believer. You see, what you believe in this life determines where you will spend the afterlife: heaven or hell. Those who believe in Christ are the true church, the bride of Christ, and have a home prepared for them in heaven. The apostle John, in Revelation 21, was summoned by an angel to get a glimpse of heaven. The angel said to John:

> 9 "Come, I will show you **the bride, the wife of the Lamb.** 10 And he carried me away in the Spirit to a mountain great and high, and showed me the Holy City, Jerusalem, coming down out of heaven from God." (Bold added)

Of course, Christ is the lamb to whom the angel was referring. This vision that the angel gave to John was followed by a detailed, fantastic description of heaven itself. Heaven is the church's new home (Revelation 21-22).

The most important point from all these parallel and prefiguring types is that God wants to redeem you. That's what God wants for every single person. It has been His desire to buy you out of your destitution and enslavement to sin and from its consequences of death. He has already paid the price with his own blood—His life for our lives. He wants to redeem you, to give you a whole new life.

All single-again people know the brutality of sin. Some know too well how harsh the sin called "hardness of heart" is. Hard heartedness was the sin, according to Jesus, that led to divorce (Matthew 19:8). The widowed single also knows too well how harsh the penalty of sin is. That penalty was death and that death initiated them into the single-again life. Most single-again people do not have to be convinced that "all have sinned." They know it. They've experienced it. The good news is that "where sin increased, grace increased all the more" (Romans 5:20). There is hope for the single-again person. That hope comes from the fact that God wants to redeem you and He wants to bless you, too.

There is hope for the single-again person. That hope comes from the fact that God wants to redeem you and He wants to bless you, too.

God Wants to Bless Your Life

That God wants to bless you is the second major premise of this final chapter of Ruth. When people pronounce a blessing, their blessing is actually a sort of prayer. Normally when you pray for someone, you take them before God by name and with some sort of positive request for them. But in a blessing you invoke God to visit the person you are blessing with some favorable circumstance. As we pick up the case study we will see that it was the elders who invoked God to bless Boaz as a husband. The elders played a larger role than just witnesses to the real estate deal. They also invoked God's blessing on Boaz as well. Elders today can play a larger part than just men with titles in the organization of your church.

When I had been single again for several years and was certain that sufficient healing had taken place in my life, I made a request of our church Elders. The church elders were the governing body at the church where I was on staff as the associate pastor. At their regular meeting they would take prayer requests and then pray for those requests before doing Elder business. As I attended the meeting, I asked the Elders to pray for me. In fact, my request was rather specific. I said, "You know that I have been single again for a number of years, and you know that I have taught divorce recovery classes constantly that whole time. I feel that sufficient time has passed for me to have healed from my past emotional and relational wounds that came with my divorce. So I would like to ask you Elders to pray that God would bring a godly woman into my life." The elders stopped the meeting after my request and began to pray for me and my specific request. Now wouldn't you know it, the very next Saturday evening, I met Dianne, whom I would later marry and who is now my godly wife.

I'm not saying that every reader of this book should clutter the elders' meetings with requests for mates. But I am saying that when you have spent years healing from your past and God has placed it in your heart to find a spouse, that the prayers of the elders are a powerful starting point. Their prayers put me in the right field to meet my Ruth and put Dianne in the right field to meet her Boaz.

So let's pick up with the Elders' prayer that we call a blessing.

11 Then the elders and all those at the gate said, "We are witnesses. May the LORD make the woman who is coming into your home like Rachel and Leah, who together built up the house of Israel. May you have standing in Ephrathah and be famous in Bethlehem. 12 Through the offspring the LORD gives you by this young woman, may your family be like that of Perez, whom Tamar bore to Judah."

The elders' blessing over Boaz had three parts. The first part of the blessing focused on Boaz' home. There may be a play on the meaning of the word "home" and "house," as reflected in the NIV Bible. Both words in verse 11 are the same Hebrew word (*bayith*). However the first usage, in all likelihood refers to Boaz' actual dwelling place—his house as his residence. The second time the word is used it seems to refer to a lineage or dynasty, as in the expression "the house of Israel." The point is God wants to bless your home.

This is important because nearly every single-again person took a huge loss with respect to their home when the divorce or death of the spouse occurred. God wants to bless you with respect to your home. The elders believed that and invoked God to do the blessing.

That the Divine Case Worker did not name the woman that was coming into Boaz' house seems rather intentional. She was only called "the woman." Of course we all know from context that "the woman" was Ruth. It seems that her name was deliberately dropped to add emphasis on the female names that were mentioned: Rachael and Leah. Because all the names so far in the book add to the storyline,

116

the question is, "What possibly could these two names add?" Rachael means "Ewe"[8] and Leah means "Weariness."[9] Strange names, no doubt. So how do they fit into the case study?

From the first passage in the Bible, where two of the names are mentioned together, we learn that they were sisters who married the same man "Jacob" (Genesis 29:16-28). Leah was the older of the two sisters, and yet in the Book of Ruth she is mentioned last. From the Genesis account we also learn that "Leah had weak eyes, but Rachel was lovely in form, and beautiful." It is all too obvious that the one called "Weariness" was a plain Jane. The best that Moses could write of her was that she had "weak eyes;" while her younger sister "Ewe" was drop dead gorgeous and took first place. Together, "Plain Jane" and "Gorgeous" gave Jacob twelve sons, from which the twelve tribes of Israel sprung (incidentally "Israel" means "God prevails"[10]). Of course, all that may be intended by the mention of these two female names is that the elders were invoking God to bless Boaz with one wife who would cover all that these two did. But with such an emphasis on names in the case study, it may be that the blessing is even richer in meaning. " May Boaz' home be blessed whatever the circumstances the future may bring; and may the God Who prevails bring blessing whether weary days or beautiful ones lie ahead." In any case, it was God's prosperity that that the elders invoked upon Boaz' home.

The second part of blessing zeroed in on Boaz' character.

May you have standing in Ephrathah and be famous in Bethlehem.

The expression "May you have standing" is literally "May you have valor" (*khayil*; valor/virtue). It is the same word used in the Hebrew "mighty man of valor!" This second part of the blessing was directed at Boaz' character. The elders invoked God to continue granting Boaz the same stuff that already made him great—valor.

The third part of the blessing concerned future offspring—a family.

12 Through the offspring the LORD gives you by this young woman, may your family be like that of Perez, whom Tamar bore to Judah."

It's not hard to see how Tamar, whose name means "palm tree" or "pillar" played into the story of Boaz and Ruth. Tamar stood her ground like a pillar, as she found herself a widow like Ruth in need of a kinsman-redeemer to father an heir. Moses recorded her plight for us in Genesis 38.

Tamar was married to Judah's first born son named Er. But Er died leaving Tamar without a child. Consequently, Judah told Onan, his next oldest son, "Lie with your brother's wife and fulfill your duty to her as a brother-in-law to produce offspring for your brother." But Onan knew that the offspring would not be his. So whenever he lay with his brother's wife, he spilled his semen on the ground. As a result, the Lord slew him.

Judah then promised that if Tamar were to wait as mourning widow that he would give her to his younger son Shelah. Shelah was too young to wed. After time had passed, Shelah grew up but Tamar was not given to him as a wife. So Tamar took matters into her own hands, much like the boldness of Naomi and Ruth who strategized a way to propose that Boaz propose to Ruth.

Tamar disguised herself as a shrine prostitute and strategically placed herself in Judah's path. The disguise worked, and Judah unwittingly slept with his daughter-in-law but had nothing with which to pay. So Tamar took his staff and his seal (the seal was equal to his signature) as a pledge that he would send payment. When Judah tried to make good on it and pay her, he could not find the shrine prostitute because Tamar had returned to her previous role of a mourning widow.

Three months later Tamar was showing that she was pregnant. Judah was outraged and demanded that she be burned for her immorality. Undaunted, like a pillar, she stood her ground, and said, "I am pregnant by the man who owns these." She then produced Judah's staff and seal. Judah finally acknowledged, "She is more righteous than I." When she gave birth, there were twin boys in her womb. The one burst out his arm, and the midwife tied a scarlet thread on it to identify him as the first born. He was then called Perez because Perez meant "burst forth."

From this we see that the blessing invoked by the elders focused on offspring. This had several layers of significance. First, Ruth, like Tamar, would have a child by an older kin of her dead husband. Second, both had a child as the result of strategizing to get one. Third, both women would become mothers in the linage of both King David and Jesus Christ (Ruth 4:12,13; 1 Chronicle 2:4; Matthew 1:3).

Well, the elders' had invoked God to bless Boaz because God is in the business of blessing His people. He not only wants to redeem you, He wants to bless you, too. He wants to bless your home, your character, and your future.

God is in the business of blessing His people. He not only wants to redeem you, He wants to bless you, too. He wants to bless your home, your character, and your future.

God Wants a Wedding Worth Waiting For

13 So Boaz took Ruth and she became his wife. Then he went to her, and the LORD enabled her to conceive, and she gave birth to a son.

This was a wedding worth waiting for. Ruth became Boaz' wife. Noteworthy is the fact that they had saved Steps

119

7-12 of Bonding a Relationship for Life for their marriage and did so with no regret. There was no guilt associated with this relationship because there was no immorality. There was no extra guilty baggage brought into the marriage.

What a honeymoon they must have had. They explored Steps 7-12 and God blessed them. Ruth conceived on her honeymoon. Nine months later she had a baby boy who would become heir to all Boaz and Ruth had. Think about it—Ruth had left Moab just a year previous to the wedding and now, nine months later, had a son. It is amazing what a year or two in God's will can do for you. So much had gone so right for Ruth since her decision to put the true and living God in her life. It is at this point we would anticipate the line, "And they lived happily ever after." And though they did live happily ever after, the case study is not over. There is still more to the story.

God Wants You To Know That There is More

In our current American culture 75 percent of all single-again people will remarry (and 75 percent of those will become single-again a second time). That means that 75 percent of the readers of this case study who are single again will remarry. It also means that 25 percent will not. The remainder of this case study is for those 25%-ers who will not remarry. If we assume that Orpah, who returned to Moab, remarried, based on Naomi's advice (Ruth 1:10), then of the four singles that were covered in this case study only one, Naomi, did not tie the knot again. She was among the 25%-ers.

75 percent of all single-again people will remarry.

To compound the issue, it appears that Boaz was actually nearer in age to Naomi than to Ruth. Boaz was, in all likelihood, Naomi's brother-in-law, perhaps Elimelech's younger brother. Furthermore, the phrase "my daughter" occurs eight times (Ruth 2:2, 8, 22; 3:1, 10, 11, 16, 18). Five times Naomi called Ruth "my daughter," and three times Boaz did also. The point is "Boaz was old enough to be Ruth's father." Can you imagine how Naomi must have felt while strategizing her "b-harmony" method to snag Boaz for Ruth? She was helping the young woman get the man who was more her own age. If we had been Naomi, we probably would have been asking, "How fair is that?" "What about me?" "Who will marry me?"

Well, the thrust of what follows is "Don't feel sorry for Naomi!" Don't feel sorry for the 25%-ers! The 25%-ers will be much happier single than they ever would be with the wrong spouse! Don't ever forget that. Let's see how this all unfolded.

God Wants You to Stop Feeling Sorry for the 25%-ers

Don't feel sorry for Naomi. The women of the "House of Bread" did not. They found Naomi's life one of inspiration and hope. They saw her life as an occasion to praise the true and living God.

14 The women said to Naomi: "Praise be to the LORD, who this day has not left you without a kinsman-redeemer. May he become famous throughout Israel! 15 He will renew your life and sustain you in your old age. For your daughter-in-law, who loves you and who is better to you than seven sons, has given him birth."

The women of Bethlehem saw Naomi's life blessed in several ways. First, the women credited her with having a kinsman-redeemer. Pity the person in our culture who does not have *the* Kinsman-Redeemer. Pity the person who does not know Jesus Christ as Savior. So what if they have a spouse—if they do not have Jesus Christ as Savior, they are to be most pitied.

Second, through Naomi's kinsman-redeemer her life was renewed. Not only was Ruth's life changed, so was Naomi's.

She had a home, she had protection, and she had a future. The blessings from Ruth's life spilled over into Naomi's life. Sometimes we forget that God can bless us through relationships that don't involve marriage.

Third, through her kinsman-redeemer her life would be sustained. One of the biggest fears singles face is that they will grow old alone. No, you don't have to. You can develop relationships with groups of singles or other married people who will sustain you as a single without marriage. Furthermore, the Bible tells us that Christ is really all we need. A relationship with Christ will sustain you when everyone else has failed you. He is the ultimate Kinsman-Redeemer.

Fourth, her daughter-in-law loved her. Do you remember when Naomi returned from Moab? (Ruth 1:21). She was convinced God had dealt with her bitterly. From her perspective, and with a little rewriting of her history, she felt that she had gone out full and had returned empty. She really hadn't. She had Ruth who loved her. The point is you don't have to be married to love or be loved!

Fifth, her daughter-in-law was better than seven sons (and that daughter-in-law had delivered a grandson). Ruth was the best thing that had happened to Naomi since her own personal experience of embracing the Lord as her Redeemer. Ruth was better than seven sons, and Naomi knew the value of a son. She had lost two.

Every single person can build non-marriage relationships that can be better than married relationships—it's true. Even guys can. Tucked away in the book of 2 Samuel is a verse that tells us that David had such a relationship with Jonathan. In his grieving over the death of his friend,

> Since every single-again person is potentially among the 25%-ers who will not remarry, then every single-again person needs to believe that with God the best is yet to come—even if you never remarry.

Jonathan, David cried out: "I grieve for you, Jonathan my brother; you were very dear to me. Your love for me was wonderful, more wonderful than that of women" (2 Samuel 1:26). There was nothing sexual about this—this was a profoundly close relationship between friends. There are friendships that can be closer than a marriage. Remind yourself of that!

Since every single-again person is potentially among the 25%-ers who will not remarry, then every single-again person needs to believe that with God the best is yet to come—even if you never remarry. It was for Naomi and we will see further how that is so.

16 Then Naomi took the child, laid him in her lap and cared for him. 17 The women living there said, "Naomi has a son."

The child was one of the best things to come into Naomi's life. Grandkids have a way of doing that. But did you notice that the women of Bethlehem called the child Naomi's "son." This is huge. When Naomi left Moab, she had told her daughters-in-law that she would not be having any sons (Ruth 1:11-13). She had limited God. But from the perspective of the women of Bethlehem, God gave her a "son." They saw all that had happened as having been governed by God's overriding hand to give her this son. This son, and all the attending circumstances that brought his life about, happened to serve a much grander purpose. That grander purpose follows.

The Grander Purpose of Living Single Again

Don't dismiss the last six verses in this case study; they contain an important genealogy. They are the apparent reason the Divine Case Worker recorded the events in this book in the first place. He was recording the legacy of Boaz and Ruth for future generations. It's here for the grander

Don't dismiss the last six verses in this case study; they contain an important genealogy. They are the apparent reason the Divine Case Worker recorded the events in this book in the first place.

purpose of focusing on the future—not the past. God worked out every event in each single person's life to bring about a baby boy who would grow up under Naomi, Ruth, and Boaz' influence. Then one day he, too, would marry to have a son. This cycle would repeat again and a king would come from this line, King David, who was perhaps the greatest King until Jesus Christ.

No matter what you're facing that may have you bitter—just remember Rom-ans 8:28 "And we know that in all things God works for the good of those who love him, who have been called according to his purpose." If you know Jesus Christ as your Savior, then your future is bright. It may not seem like it in the present but something grander awaits you.

17 And they named him Obed. He was the father of Jesse, the father of David. 18 This, then, is the family line of Perez: Perez was the father of Hezron, 19 Hezron the father of Ram, Ram the father of Amminadab, 20 Amminadab the father of Nahshon, Nahshon the father of Salmon, 21 Salmon the father of Boaz, Boaz the father of Obed, 22 Obed the father of Jesse, and Jesse the father of David.

For the first time the name of Ruth and Boaz' son is given. They named him "Obed." As with all Biblical names there is a meaning. And, of course, the meaning has significance within the story. The name "Obed" meant "servant, worshipper." [11] When "Friendship" and "Strength" (Ruth and Boaz) had a son, they named him "Worshipper."

Could it be that they earnestly desired that this son would grow up to be a servant of the Lord and a true worshipper of God?

Well, according to this genealogy Obed, "the worshipper," had a son named Jesse, which means "hold out, extend"[12] and may suggest "give a gift." He had a son named David, which means "Beloved."[13] Could it be that worship involves a gift given from love? Now the text does not come out and say this; we only surmise this by reading between the lines.

What the text actually wants us to know is that Ruth and Boaz are the great-grandparents of King David, God's beloved, "a man after God's own heart" (1 Samuel 13:14). We should draw from this that each of us is leaving a legacy. How we handle our "single again-ness" and future relationships may impact generations yet to come.

At verse 18 the Divine Case Worker gives a detailed genealogy that goes back to Judah's son Perez (both Judah and Perez were mentioned in the blessing of the Elders found in verse 4:12). All the names in this genealogy have meanings. How they connect with or contribute to the case study can only be surmised. The text does not give us an authoritative connection. Here are the names and meanings:

> Perez means "Burst forth."
> Hezron means "Enclosure"
> Ram means "Highly exalted."
> Amminadab means "My kinsman is noble."
> Nashon means "Divination."
> Salmon means "Garment."
> Boaz means "Strength."
> Obed means "Worshipper."
> Jesse means "Hold out."
> David means "Beloved."[14]

Perhaps, and only perhaps, a Hebrew-listening audience would have known the meaning of all these Hebrew names.

Perhaps they would have read between the lines and come up with a message. Perhaps knowing that the first person mentioned, Perez, was fathered by Judah (which means "praise") they may have connected the dots like this: "Praise" the God who "bursts forth" to "protect (or enclose)." My "highly exalted" One provided "my noble kinsman." He "discerns the future" and "clothed" himself with "strength," "worship," "grace" and "love." Of course, this is only a long-shot guess.

The real point of the passage is that God had been providentially working in every detail of all these men's lives. Every detail, good and bad, contributed to bringing them into relationships that brought about the next generation. There were no accidents—only Divine appointments. Even what appeared to be bad, God orchestrated into His grander purpose. You see, God in His sovereignty orchestrated all the events of the ten generations to bring on the scene the king after God's own heart: King David. He didn't stop there. Matthew 1:1-21 contains another genealogy that picks up with David and ends with Jesus, the Christ.

All the pain you've experienced will somehow be used by God for a grander purpose. He will not waste any of it. You can be sure of that. Since that is so, you can trust and praise God for it!

Here's the point for the single-again person. Your circumstances, good or bad, are being orchestrated by God to accomplish a much grander purpose that you may not even see in your lifetime. All the pain you've experienced will somehow be used by God for a grander purpose. He will not waste any of it. You can be sure of that. Since that is so, you can trust and praise God for it!

Conclusion:

Famines are unavoidable. Famines are unpredictable, too. As I mentioned at the beginning of this case study, when I pulled into my driveway, with the sound of crushing gravel under my tires, and paused to thank God for all His blessing in my life—I did not know that in less than 12 months I would have the famine of all famines in my life up to that point. I could not have predicted it. I did not expect it. I did not want it. I certainly could not avoid it. You never know when famine will hit or where they will hit. There are some things in life you just have no control over—famine, war, terrorism, hurricanes, tornados, drought, pestilence, the stock market, cancer, heart disease, death, and many times a divorce.

You cannot control the famine in life produced by such events, but you can control how you respond to them. That's what this case study has taught. There are no "time-outs" in life. You have to make choices even when famine strikes. "Will I stay and endure the famine" (like Boaz) or "Will I flee to escape it" (like Elimelech). Of course, to flee is only to find one's self in another place and another time, facing a famine of another kind. That's what happened to Naomi. The grass only appeared greener on the other side. Perhaps you need to begin, right now, accepting your circumstances as part of God's almighty providential hand that is working in your life in such a way that will ultimately lead to His greatest glory. Trust Him through the famine instead of avoiding the famine.

When a "relationship famine" strikes, like death and divorce that separates people from previous relationships, there are basically three choices to be made in life. You can turn your back on God and go back to an old life-style; you can turn bitter against God over the new single-again life-style; or you can get better from the lessons God will teach you through the crisis. This case study showed all three of these choices and that "getting better" is the only wise choice. That's what Ruth did and what Naomi eventually did. No matter what you are facing right now, choose to get better!

It is so hard to choose to get better when writhing from the anguish of a recent, devastating divorce or death of a loved one. At that time you are overwhelmingly convinced that life is a curse; that attitude only leads to bitterness just as it did for Naomi who called herself "Marah" (Bitter). Life's circumstances can be so severe that you just want to die as well. However, whether the crisis is really a curse or blessing is something that only time will tell. You see, God is in the business of turning curses into blessings and ultimately "God works for the good of those who love him, who have been called according to his purpose" (Romans 8:28).

God knows what every single person wants before he or she does. He knows what you want before you do, too. You can trust Him on that. This case study taught that every single godly woman, deep inside, desires a man like Boaz, a "mighty man of valor" who was strong on the inside. That inner strength enabled him to confront the famine of life and overcome it. Nothing has changed. Godly women today desire the same qualities that a "mighty man of valor" has. Women want a man with inner strength, who has eyes only for her, who is gracious, who comforts her, who engages in heart talk with her, who protects her, and provides for her. Men today need to focus on themselves and endeavor to be such a man.

Likewise, what every single godly man is looking for is a woman like Ruth, a beautiful "woman of virtue," who is beautiful on the inside. She had that inner beauty of the soul that trusted God to overcome the famines of life. Nothing has changed. Godly men today still want a virtuous woman who respects him, who accepts him the way he is, who is equal to him, who believes in him, and who is patient with him. Women today need to focus on themselves and endeavor to become such woman.

The case study has asked, "What if when you find that

'man of valor' or 'woman of virtue' that your heart longs for, but that person does not find you to be such a 'woman of virtue' or 'man of valor?'" Or what if while you are settling for less and dating the less than desirable, the "man of valor" or "woman of virtue" comes along and assesses you to be "already taken" by the undesirable? Don't settle for less than God's best for your life. Since God already knows what you want, wait on Him.

This case study was clear about what God wants for every single person. He wants to both redeem and bless you. He has already paid the purchase price to make you His own. It was Christ Who paid the price of our sins, that price was death. Jesus died as a substitute in the guilty sinner's place. So every single person needs to call on Him to save and deliver him or her from the mess he or she has made of life. Acknowledge that you have sinned and that life is a mess. Then ask Him to save you from it. He will. He is mighty to save. He wants to save you now.

He also wants to bless you. This case study emphasized that He wants to bless your own personal character, your home, and your family. Why would you not want that? Turn to Him and live for Him—He wants to bless you.

Blessing you may not result in another marriage. The truth is 75 percent of all single-again people will remarry. That means 25 percent will not. Those 25%-ers are not to be pitied because a person can be more content single, and not married, than the person who has married the wrong person. Marriage of itself does not make anyone happy. You can learn to be happy and satisfied with yourself, by yourself. You choose to make yourself happy. That is an important lesson to learn. Remind yourself of it.

The last lesson of this study is that even as a single person you are not to live for self. Your single life influences other peoples' lives—other singles and married people, your family members, and most of all your children and grandchildren. You are leaving a legacy. What will those who come behind your "single life" say about you? Will they say, "He was such a man of valor" or "She was such a woman of virtue?" What will your children say? What will your grandchildren say? Leave a legacy that says, "You were all that God intended you to be." That will be enough.

Chapter Four Notes

[1] The Hebrew word "redeem" גאל (*goel*) has the basic idea of "doing the part of a kinsman who recovers property which has passed into another's hands." This required repurchasing the property. The term "goel" is used in four situations in the Old Testament: one, for purchased property that had passed into another's hands (Lev 25:25); two, for the purchase of an animal that was required to be sacrificed with another at additional cost (Lev 27:11); three, avenging a death of a relative—more or less a "pay back" (Numbers 35:12); and four, God's work to redeem Israel for His people. In all of the above, there was a price to be paid in a purchase transaction, even though the text rarely mentions the price.

[2] The year of Jubilee occurred every 50 years and included regulations on several areas of life. The most noteworthy to Naomi's and Ruth's situation were the regulations on real estate transactions. Land sold under the Old Testament economy was never ultimately sold. It was, more or less, like our modern concept of "leasing property" for up to a maximum of 50 years (until the next year of Jubilee). In the year of Jubilee, all land went back to the original owner. So even though Elimelech and Naomi had sold their land, in the year of Jubilee it would revert back to them. The next year of Jubilee would determine "when" Naomi would get the land back. If the last Year of Jubilee occurred just 10 years prior, or just before they sold their property, as they left for Moab, then the next Year of Jubilee would come as late as 40 years from her present distressing circumstances. That would mean in 40 years the land would go back to Naomi. Of course, if the last year of Jubilee was 49 years ago, then the next one would come as soon as the next year, and the land would revert back to her then. In either case, whether the year of Jubilee would occur the next year or 40 years from then, the nearest kinsman-redeemer had the right to buy it back immediately.

[3] Leviticus 25:13-17.

[4] Deuteronomy 25:7 legislated that the town elders were to be witnesses of the levirate marriage. Since Boaz really wanted Ruth for his wife (the purchase of the land was only incidental), he summoned the elders. The number of elders who sat as witnesses was not prescribed by the law. However, for serious judgments three would be necessary, as Deuteronomy 19:15 states: "One witness is not enough to convict a man accused of any crime or offense he may have committed. A matter must be established by the testimony of two or three witnesses." Although no crime is involved in Ruth 4 the precedent appears to have been set for the need of witnesses for other kinds of legal transactions as well.

[5] NET Bible, the Book of Ruth, Chapter four, verse 9, sn (Study Note) 9 (http://www.bible.org/netbible/).

[6] The ethical question is often raised, "What if the nearest kinsman-redeemer was already married? Would he be obligated to take his brother's widow as wife? Would this not lead to incest and/or polygamy?" John McArthur succinctly responds to this in his study Bible notes: "God would not design a good plan to involve the grossest of immoralities punishable by death. It is to be assumed that the implementation of Deut. 25:5,6 could involve only the nearest relative who was eligible for marriage as qualified by other stipulations of the law." (*The MacArthur Study Bible*, Word, 1997, p.367). Based on this truth, it appears that the nearer kinsman-redeemer was also single or single again. Either he had never married, was a widower, or had been divorced. In all likelihood, he was widowed and already had children whose inheritance would have been in jeopardy. However, if he had never been married then it would have been the inheritance of future children that he wanted to protect.

[7] The Greek New Testatment's single word τετελεσται (*tetelestai*) is rendered by the phrase "It is finished." The verb ...was used in the first and second centuries in the sense of "fulfilling" or "paying" a debt and often appeared on receipts. Jesus' statement "It is finished" ... could be interpreted as "Paid in full"....

(Merrill Tenny, *The Expositior's Bible Commentary: John*, 1981, vol. 9, note 30, p. 185).

8 The name "Rachael" רחל (*Rachel*) was derived from the word that meant "ewe" (BDB p. 932).

9 The name "Leah" לאה (*Leah*) was derived from the word that meant "weariness, hardship" (BDB p. 521).

10 The name "Israel" ישראל (*Israel*) was derived from the word that meant "persist, persevere" (BDB p.975). The name is first used in Genesis 32:28, "Then the man said, 'Your name will no longer be Jacob, but Israel, because you have struggled with God and with men and have overcome.'"

11 The name "Obed" עובד (*Obed*) was derived from the word that meant "worshipper, serve" (BDB p. 714).

12 The name "Jesse" ישי (*Yese*) was derived from the word that meant "hold out" (as in extending a scepter--BDB p. 445).

13 The name "David" דוד (David) was derived from the word that meant "beloved" (BDB p.187).

14 Below are charted the names according BDB, TWOT, and Gesenius.

English Name	Hebrew Word	Meaning	Source
Perez	פרץ	"burst forth, breech"	BDB p. 829
Hezron	חצרון	"enclosure"	TWOT Vol 1, p.720
Ram	רם	"highly exalted"	BDB p. 928
Amminadab	עמינדב	"my kinsman is noble"	BDB p. 770
Nashon	נחשון	"divination, fortune telling"	BDB p. 638

Salmon	שׁלמה	"garment"	Gesenius p. 791
Boaz	בעז	"strength"	BDB p. 127
Obed	עובד	"worshipper"	BDB p. 714
Jesse	ישׁי	"hold out, extend"	BDB p. 445
David	דוד	"beloved"	BDB p.187

Addendum

Small Group Study Questions

The following pages are questions intended for small group discussion or for individual personal study.

Small group facilitator help is available online at:

http://www.OLordImSingleAgain.com/facilitator.htm

Questions for Chapter One of Ruth

1. Do you know what your name means? If so, share that with us. If not, find out so you can share it with us the next time we meet. Can you think of some way your name reflects your character?

2. Do you think the famine in the case study occurred as punishment, chastisement, or just coincidentally? Why? How do you view the famines in your life?

3. What was the most painful part of your becoming single again?

4. Have you known anyone who made a start in recovery, but dropped out? If so, where are they today?

5. It was mentioned that some people are like Orpah, who "went back." Today, what do people "go back" to?

6. Ruth converted to the faith as a result of living single again. How has your reentry into the single-again life changed your spiritual journey?

7. Ruth entered a promissory covenant with Naomi that she would be there for her. So how could we make a similar covenant promise within our single-again journey?

8. Naomi became bitter and seemed to blame it on God. Have you played the blame game? If so, over what? Who really makes us bitter? Why?

9. Have you heard the fable of "Curse or Blessing" before? How does the fable make you feel about your current circumstances?

10. What will you change in your life as a result of this lesson?

Questions for Chapter Two of Ruth

1. If you did not know what your name meant after lesson one and looked it up, share with us what your name means.

2. God interrupted the Case Study to let us know that He already knew what Ruth was looking for—do you believe He already knows who is best for you, too? If so, how might believing that change the way you live?

3. From Ruth's perspective, that day of looking for work was just another routine day in her life of trying to survive—but "As it turned out, she found herself working in a field belonging to Boaz." How might that help us face this next week?

4. From your perspective, when approaching "dating," do men focus more on the "mighty man" or on the "valorous man?" How does it show up? Why do they do what they do?

5. Do you agree that "every single godly woman wants a mighty man of valor?" How about "a man with a heart?" How about "a man of commitment?" What do those words mean to YOU?

6. Ruth wanted to be noticed, and Boaz noticed her. Obviously it meant more than answering the question, "Oh, did you see that woman?" with a trite, "I saw someone—but really didn't pay much attention."
   So how do godly women want to be noticed today? What really makes them feel "noticed?"

7. The 12 Steps of bonding were super-imposed onto the Book of Ruth—do you think it was a stretch? If so, how? If not, why not?

8. It was suggested that the turning point for Naomi from "Bitterness" back to "My Pleasantness" took place when she discovered that God placed Ruth in Boaz' field. What was your turning point from bitterness or anger? Or are you still

looking for that event?

9. Who seems most interested in the other at this point in the Case Study? Was Boaz more interested in Ruth or was Ruth more interested in Boaz? Were both mutually interested? Were both not interested at all?
In your last relationship who was more interested, you or the other person?

10. Was God really interested in who they met? If so, is God really interested in who you date? If so, in what areas of dating?

11. How might this lesson change the way you date?

Questions for Chapter Three of Ruth

1. Is there a difference between a godly man saying that he wants a "beautiful woman of virtue" and others who say the same thing?
Are all professing "Christian" men godly?
How does a godly man show what he wants?

2. It was suggested that a virtuous woman is both *submissive* and *respectful*.
How do you feel about that?
What do those terms mean to you?
Why would a long and slow dating process be beneficial in this area?

3. Naomi and Ruth were *submissive* and yet *assertive*.
How do you feel about a woman asking a man out on a date?
How do you feel about a woman proposing marriage to a man?

4. It was suggested that a virtuous woman *accepts* the man.
What one item did Ruth have to accept about Boaz?
Should age, race, or status hinder a relationship?
What's the difference between accepting a guy and having boundaries that exclude a guy?

5. It was suggested that a virtuous woman is *equal to* the man. How so? How are they different?

6. It was suggested that a virtuous woman *believes* in her man and that obstacles come along to test her trust.
   What can a woman do to not loose faith or to restore faith in a man?
   What can a man do to promote or restore faith in him?

7. It was suggested that a virtuous woman is *patient* with her man.
   What does patience imply?
   How long should one wait for a commitment to the relationship?
   Why would a long engagement be a bad thing?

8. It appears Ruth and Boaz saved Steps 7-12 for marriage.
   Is that reasonable for our day?
   At which step will you draw the line? Why?

9. The thrust of this lesson was to focus on yourself. After all, "What if when you find that 'Person of Valor/Virtue,' they don't find YOU to be one?"
   What are you going to do to focus on YOU?

Questions for Chapter Four of Ruth

1. How does the teaching that God wants to redeem you and to bless you make you feel?

2. How might really believing that "God owns all that you have and all that you are" change your life-style?

3. Boaz had a strategy to accomplish his goal. Sum up his strategy the best you can. So how does having a strategy complement trusting God for future relationships?

4. It was suggested that God wants to both redeem you and your possessions. What have you lost that you hope to get back?

5. The elders blessed Boaz and Ruth, and that blessing was important to them. So whose blessing is important to you? Who would you like to share your important prayer requests with?

6. The elders blessed Boaz in three areas:
   1) His house
   2) His character
   3) His future
   In what area do you want His blessing the *most*? Why?

7. Boaz and Ruth saved Steps 7-12 for marriage.
   What is the wisdom in doing that?
   What is the drawback?

8. It was said that the 25%-ers will be happier single than with the wrong person! Do you agree or disagree? Why?
   What if it were you who is to be the 25%-er? Can you accept that?

9. It was suggested that even for the 25%-ers that the best was yet to come. Do you believe that? If so, how does that affect your life?

10. God wants to bless your legacy. What do you want most to leave behind to your children and grandchildren? Why?

Works Cited

Brown Driver and Briggs (BDB), *Hebrew and English Lexicon of the Old Testament.* Oxford: Claredon Press, 1974.

Eggerichs , Emmerson, *Love & Respect.* Brentwood, TN: Integrity, 2004.

Gesenius, *Hebrew and Chaldee Lexicon.* Grand Rapids: Eerdmans, 1971.

Glueck, Nelson, *Hesed in the Bible.* KTAV Publishing House, Inc., 1975.

Harris, Archer, and Walke, *Theological Wordbook of the Old Testament* (TWOT). 2 Vols. Chicago: Moody Press, 1980.

Henderson, Dennis, *Living Single Again*, DVD Video Series. Brighton, MI: Single Initiative, 2005.

Joy, Donald, *Bonding Relationships in the Image of God.* Waco Texas: Word Books, 1985.

Kübler-Ross, *On Death and Dying.* New York: Macmillan Publihing Co., 1969.

Labi, Nadya, "A Bad Start," *Time*, February 15, 1999.

Lucado, Max, http://www.maxlucado.com/read/woodcutter/index2.html.

MacArthur, John, *The John MacArthur Study Bible.* Nashville: Word, 1997.

Morris, Desmond, *Intimate Behavior.* New York: Random House, 1971.

New English Bible, The Book of Ruth, Study Notes on Ruth, http://www.bibleorg/netbible.

Tenny, Merrill, *The Expositior's Bible Commentary: John.* Vol. 9. Grand
     Rapids: Zondervan 1981.

Wood, Leon, *Distressing Days of the Judges.* Grand Rapids:
     Zondervan, 1975.

Wright, Norman, *Relationships that Work: (and Those That Don't).*
     Ventura, CA: Regal Books, 1998.

More studies by Dr. Dennis Henderson

LIVING™
Single Again

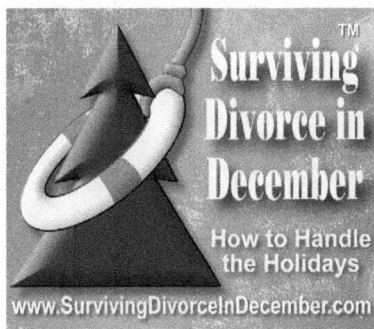

143